THE VOICES OF
NEGRO PROTEST IN AMERICA

THE VOICES OF
NEGRO PROTEST IN
AMERICA

W. HAYWOOD BURNS

WITH A FOREWORD BY
JOHN HOPE FRANKLIN

Issued under the auspices of the
Institute of Race Relations, London

OXFORD UNIVERSITY PRESS
NEW YORK   LONDON

LC no. 63-6378
64-6467
PRINTED IN THE UNITED STATES OF AMERICA

To

BETTYE and STERLING

for different reasons

FOREWORD

THE years since the close of the Second World War have witnessed a remarkably intensive and uncompromising demand for racial equality throughout the world. The victory of the Allies over the racism of Hitler soon went far beyond the expectations, or even the hopes, of those responsible for the defeat of Aryan and other racist doctrines. With the achievement of what seemed to be a complete victory, Asians and Africans alike could challenge with impunity the assumptions of racial superiority that all too frequently formed the basis for the colonialism of Hitler's conquerors. The successful challenge of these assumptions led directly to the collapse of most of the European empires in Asia and Africa; and it contributed greatly to the intensification of the protest of Negro Americans against their mistreatment and degradation that had gone on for centuries.

It is well to remember, as Mr. Burns reminds us in the following pages, that as far as Negro Americans are concerned, the Second World War did not begin the protest for them. It merely facilitated its transition to a new, more impatient and uncompromising stage. Mr. Burns has provided his readers with a background and historical perspective so necessary to understanding the mood and method of Negro Americans as they protest today to all Americans against the shabby treatment they have received. These pages reveal how Negroes in the United States have used with great effectiveness the moral advantage they enjoy. In doing so they have forced their own country, through the courts, to recognise its own obligation to live under the law of equality that is its own creation.

The story that Mr. Burns tells is at once tragic and inspiring. Its tragedy is revealed in the unwillingness of vast numbers of white Americans to accept their own doctrines of equality as set forth in the Declaration of Independence and the Constitution of the United States. White Citizens' Councils, the Ku Klux Klan, ingenious evasions of the law and of court orders, and the not infrequent resort to violence are painful reminders of the extent to which millions of white Americans are committed to a barbarism that involves the worship of a value as specious and worthless as the colour of one's skin. But the story is also inspiring, as one reads of the persistent, uncompromising determination of Negroes to secure their rights by forcing their country, where they have lived longer than most white Americans, to live by their own doctrines of equality. In the middle of the twentieth century Negroes in the United States are impatient and defiant; some of them have even resorted to a racism that resembles that of their white compatriots. Even that, however, reveals a vitality and a resourcefulness that will not permit any half-way solution of the problem.

Readers of this volume will doubtless have a clearer understanding of the dominant currents present in the struggle to secure racial equality in the United States and of the forces there and elsewhere that are affecting its outcome. This is, therefore, a timely and valuable statement. It wisely suggests no solution, for that would require a wisdom of which no mortal man could boast. But in its very presentation it implies the urgent necessity for an honest and diligent search for a solution. And Mr. Burns appreciates, as any thoughtful person today would appreciate, the fact that all persons everywhere should be constantly searching for and working toward the solution of this problem. He knows, as all who claim a stake in the future of civilised man know, that the solution of the race problem in the United States and the world over is one of man's greatest tests in his claim that he is truly civilised.

JOHN HOPE FRANKLIN

CONTENTS

INTRODUCTION

IN his classic study *An American Dilemma*, Gunnar Myrdal concluded his chapter on 'The Negro Protest' with a prophecy that the years following the Second World War would see increased ferment and protest in the Negro community. Since 1945 this relatively safe prognostication has been more than borne out as increasingly the Negro has demanded what he believes to be his rightful place in American life. However, more significant perhaps than the mere fact of increased protest has been the advent of new forms of protest. The use of non-violent direct action on a large scale has risen to take its place in the field of Negro protest along with the more traditional techniques. The burgeoning black nationalist sect of the Nation of Islam has shown the United States a genuine separationist movement, unique in its vehemence for white America. There is widespread evidence among many American Negroes of dissatisfaction with the traditional means of expressing grievance and seeking redress. It is my purpose in this study to investigate the important changes that Negro protest has undergone in recent years and to relate them to the total picture of Negro protest throughout American history as well as to the more immediate forces that have caused them.

In doing this, I have elected to put the whole work in historical perspective by first discussing the forms of Negro protest in the past, before passing on to a more detailed discussion of Negro protest since the Second World War. The main part of this work consists of a discussion of the traditional forms of protest as carried out by the National Association for the Advancement of Colored People in the years after the Second World War, and of two new types of protest that have arisen to challenge the traditional approach —the non-violent direct-action movement and the Black Muslim movement. Having presented the work of the

N.A.A.C.P. in recent years, I discuss these two other movements as examples of the breakdown of faith in the traditional forms of Negro protest and the search for new
approaches.

I realise some of the danger involved in writing contemporary history, but the Negro has made so much history
in the post-Second World War period that it cannot be
ignored, waiting for time to select the sources and documents
that will prove the most authoritative in giving an estimation of this period. Of necessity, I have had to base many
of my conclusions on personal contact and original research.
In arriving at an understanding of the history, philosophy
and institutional structure of the Black Muslims, for
example, I have had to depend largely on original research
and first-hand observation, since no comprehensive study
of the movement was available until the publication of
C. Eric Lincoln's *The Black Muslims in America* in 1961. In
addition to the source material of Muslim newspapers,
magazines and pamphlets, I have spent quite a lot of time
among the Black Muslim communities of Boston, New
York and Chicago. I have attended temple meetings, eaten
in Muslim restaurants, visited Muslim neighbourhoods,
talked with Muslim leaders and followers. It is from this
wealth of contacts and personal observations that much of
the information on the Muslims in this study has been
garnered.

The historian is a student of change. In recent years,
changes in the patterns of Negro protest have been taking
place with great rapidity. I have gone to some of those
behind these changes to increase my understanding of recent
developments and better to relate them to the history of
Negro protest in America in general. I am particularly
grateful for the co-operation and assistance I have received
from: James Farmer, Director of the Congress of Racial
Equality; William H. Larkins, Public Relations Department of the Congress of Racial Equality; Mrs. Constance
Baker Motley, Counsel for the N.A.A.C.P.; Miss Virginia

Breezington of the N.A.A.C.P. Research Department; Whitney Young, Director of the Urban League; Edward Cooper, Executive Secretary of the Boston N.A.A.C.P.; Dr. E. U. Essien-Udom, formerly of Harvard, now of Brown University; Minister Malcolm X. Shabazz of Muhammad's Temple 7 in New York City; Ministers Louis X. and Rodney X. of Muhammad's Temple 11 in Boston.

I owe an especially large debt of gratitude to Professor William R. Taylor, formerly at Harvard University and now Professor of History at the University of Wisconsin, who acted as my supervisor during much of this research; and to James H. Laue, former research student in Social Relations at Harvard University, currently an Assistant Professor of Sociology at Hollins College, Roanoke, Virginia. Mr. Laue began research on the sit-in movement directly after it started and has been in close contact with it ever since. Through his intensive systematic research he probably now knows more about the sit-in movement than any other person. The worth of his authority is attested to in the fact that on occasion the Reverend Dr. Martin Luther King, Jr., non-violent protest leader, has sought information from him on the non-violent movement. Mr. Laue's suggestions and criticism were especially appreciated in the writing of my chapter on non-violent direct-action protest. Throughout the creation of this work, he has proved a valuable mentor, adviser and friend.

May 1963

THE VOICES OF
NEGRO PROTEST IN AMERICA

I. ECHOES

Forms of American Negro Protest in the Past

DEPRIVATION has been a constant which the Negro in America has had to face from the time of his arrival on these shores as an unwilling immigrant to the present day. The ways in which he has responded to this deprivation have been many and varied. Under slavery, the choice for the slave lay between striking out for complete freedom or acquiescing in some way and accommodating himself to the system. Temporary accommodation in the hope of future betterment and outright agitation for full equality continued to be the alternative forms of protest in the years following emancipation. Other forms and variants of protest also appear as we move into the twentieth century. There is the birth of black nationalism among the Negro masses, and a proposed protest march that presages the birth of the non-violent direct-action approach. It is the purpose of this chapter to discuss the forms that Negro protest had taken up until the end of the Second World War and to provide the historical backdrop for the ensuing discussion of the important changes in the forms of Negro protest after the war.

Slave Revolts and Plantation Protest

During the years of American Negro slavery, there is record of over 200 slave plots and revolts.[1] The significant fact about protest under slavery, however, is not that open rebellion did occur, but that it took place so infrequently.

[1] Herbert Aptheker, *American Negro Slave Revolts*, p. 162. Aptheker has documentation for this number, but fear of slave rebellion was so great that the white populace often conjured up stories, especially in the press, of slave plots when in fact none could be found to exist. See Stanley M. Elkins, *Slavery: A Problem in American Institutional and Intellectual Life*, pp. 218–222. This figure also lacks the number of slave revolts and plots which, owing to censorship and absence of record-keeping, can never be documented.

Two hundred slave plots and revolts is not a very high number, considering that American chattel slavery lasted more than two centuries, that it flourished in an area from Maryland to Texas, that it involved millions of slaves, and that 'plots' were often the products of the over-active fears and imaginations of the whites.

Men like Gabriel Prosser, Denmark Vesey and Nat Turner were genuine protest leaders. They came forward to proclaim the cause of the masses of Negroes and were willing to translate their faith in the Negro's right to freedom into bold and decisive action. Those that followed these men, and the leaders of slave revolts that came before and after them, shared the hope for a better day and the courage to help make it. They also often shared the fate that awaited Prosser, Vesey, Turner and other slave leaders—death at the hands of the white masters.

But unlike these earliest of protest leaders, the vast majority of slaves did not actively and openly rebel against the system that was imposed upon them. Instead they accommodated and adjusted to the condition in which they found themselves. This adjustment had little, if anything, to do with whether the Negro 'liked' his status, but with whether he had any other real choice.

The institution of American chattel slavery was unique in its absolute, authoritarian character. The slave was absolutely powerless and without any rights. There were no gradations or degrees of servitude—one was either free or slave, a person with rights or a piece of property. Under conditions of such complete power and such utter domination, the slave had little choice but acquiescence. Those who rebelled against the system were mercilessly put down and their rebellion only brought in its wake harsher regimentation.[2] This fact is the background for the theory of many white liberals and accommodating Southern Negro

[2] The way in which the Turner Rebellion was put down and the reaction to it throughout the South is the best example of this. (Aptheker, *op. cit.*, pp. 300-324.)

leaders, according to which everything which arouses the resistance of the whites will deteriorate the Negro's position, so reforms must be pushed through quietly and in such a way that whites hardly notice them until they are accomplished facts engrained in a new *status quo*.[3]

The existence of so little outright protest under slavery is better understood by looking further into the status of the slave. For the slave there was no 'significant other'[4] to which he could turn except the slavemaster. Under the American form of slavery the institution of the family did not function according to traditional patterns. The natural father was denied his position as head of the household; the only provider whom the slave knew was his master. The master was source of all privilege and all punishment. Finding himself from birth in such an utterly dependent relationship and faced with grave consequences should he ever try to alter his situation, the slave could do little but accept his status and adjust himself to it. With the master his sole benefactor (however great or small) and having no other important person in his life experience for reference, it was often possible for a slave to love his master, while hating slavery.

Protest under slavery was also less possible because the slave had no institutional foundation on which to build it. Religion, education and public assembly were all rigorously controlled by the masters. Slaves could not assemble unless there were a white man present. Educating a slave was often a criminal offence. When rebellion did come, it was usually led by someone who had had a greater degree of freedom and wider exposure to the world than an ordinary field hand—Denmark Vesey was a free man who had purchased his own freedom, Nat Turner a slave preacher who had been more mobile than most slaves.

Although there were millions of slaves who made no effort at any type of overt protest, this by no means indicates an

[3] Gunnar Myrdal, *An American Dilemma*, p. 736.
[4] This is a term used by Elkins, *op. cit.*, pp. 120–23, and *passim*.

acceptance of their position as immutable or incapable of amelioration. Slaves who were unable to make the 'liberty or death' commitment to open revolt nevertheless developed their own system of protest, peculiarly adapted to the system of chattel slavery under which they lived. Through a type of 'passive rebellion' they registered their dissatisfaction with this system, and provided avenues of relief for themselves from its rigours. This more subtle and passive protest included intentional 'tool breaking' and the 'slow down'. A system of plantation ethics sprang up as a direct response to the slaves' condition. These ethics were protectionist in nature and reflected a tacit agreement among the slaves to non-cooperation with the plantation authority. Thus it was all right for slaves to steal or to lie, as long as they did not steal from or lie to each other.

Negro Protest in the North During Slavery

In the North, the free Negro sued for the full exercise of his rights and actively engaged in campaigns for the freeing of his Southern brother. Much of Northern Negro protest before the Civil War was voiced through the Convention Movement. Large groups of free Negroes gathered in Northern cities to express their grievances and to petition state legislatures and Congress for redress.[5] Their leaders spoke out and wrote against slavery and against the colonisation schemes of the American Colonisation Society and other similar groups. As early as 1817, 3,000 Negroes met in Philadelphia in a convention to protest at colonisation. The convention as a formal means of expressing grievance spread to free Negroes in other cities throughout the North with great rapidity and many cities continued to hold conventions even after the Civil War. The Convention Movement was a significant form of protest in that it represented an early attempt on the part of Negroes to organise among themselves and to petition the larger white community for redress of

[5] Howard Bell, 'Expressions of Negro Militancy in the North, 1840–1860'.

grievances through legislative action and change in public policy.

Another important form of Negro protest in the North during this period is represented by the Negro abolitionists. It was with men like Frederick Douglass, Charles Ray, Robert Purvis, Lunsford Lane, and women like Sojurner Truth that for the first time the Negro personally argued his case before large white audiences. Douglass, a runaway slave who had come to Massachusetts, was by far the most outstanding of these Negro abolitionists. His career as a leader of Negro protest carries over into the post-Civil War period when he was regarded as the spokesman for the Negro in America.

Prosser, Vesey and Turner had felt that a call to arms was the solution to the slave's problems. When the nation itself went to war against the slave power, Negroes joined in the struggle. Once the Negro was permitted to enlist in the Northern army, he did so and served with valour and distinction, both behind and in the lines. There were 186,000 Negroes who enlisted in the Union army, 133,000 of these from Southern and border states. At least 38,000 Negroes gave their lives as a final protest against that 'peculiar institution' which had so long bound them and their kinsmen.

Exodus

In the years following the Civil War, the Negro in the South found it difficult to adjust to the new way of life and found that freedom often took a form he had not expected. With the return of the ex-Confederates to power, the Negro's position, far from ameliorated, was even more intolerable. His solution to these difficulties, he felt, was to leave. The year 1879 marks the beginning of a large-scale exodus of Negroes from the South into the North and West—especially Kansas. Leaders of these 'exodusters', as they were called, were Henry Adams of Louisiana and another Negro, Benjamin 'Pap' Singleton of Tennessee. Adams claimed to have organised 98,000 Negroes to go West. It is more likely, however, that this is the number of persons expressing a willingness to go whose names he managed to collect. Singleton's writings and exhortations influenced thousands more.[6]

Whites became alarmed at the loss of great numbers of their labourers and sought to stem the tide of the exodus in order that the Negro might be kept in the South, in the fields. The enforcement of vagrancy and labour contract laws, enactment of laws punishing those who enticed labourers away and the establishment of Negro peonage systems were all calculated to 'keep the Negro where he belonged'.

Migration from the area of oppression has since been the way in which the Negro has shown his discontent and sought to better his condition. Throughout most of this century large-scale Negro migration from the South has been a constant phenomenon. In 1910, 81 per cent of the nation's Negro population lived in the states of the old Confederacy; but by 1960 this had dropped to only slightly more than half. Of course, motivations for migration are complex and it has not been Negroes alone who have been in motion. There has been a shifting of the white population also in the same period, but not nearly as much or with as much of a South-to-North trend. Since the economic motivation which is so important in this migration is so intimately bound up with the Negro's racial and social situation it is difficult to allot the proper amount of influences to each, but the importance of racial deprivation as a contributing factor must not be minimised. Migration was first accepted as a solution by those Negroes who had decided to take part in the colonisation schemes of the earlier nineteenth century. At different times and in different forms this alternative was to come up again in the history of the Negro in America.

[6] Ray Garvin, 'Benjamin, or "Pap" Singleton and His Followers', *The Journal of Negro History*, XXXIII, January 1948, pp. 7–23. Also see Glen Schwendermann, 'St. Louis and the "Exodusters" of 1879', *The Journal of Negro History*, XLVI, January 1961.

Colored Farmers' Alliance

The Colored Farmers' National Alliance and Co-operative Union was formed in 1886. Its formation was only part of an even larger wave of radical agrarian reform that was sweeping the South and parts of the West at this time. By 1890 the Colored Farmers' Alliance claimed a member-ship of 1 million Negroes. A major part of the significance of this Negro farmers' movement lies in the way in which it aligned with Southern white farmers' groups in the cause of agrarian reform.

The brief *entente* of the Negro farmer and the white farmer in the cause of Populism during the early 1890s represents the closest that Southerners have come to unifying in a common cause without regard to race. Southern Populists denounced the lynch law and the convict lease system. They called for the defence of the Negro's political rights, and extended political privilege and recognition to the Negroes within the party. Before the reversion to white supremacy in the later 1890s gains were made in the area of rights for Negroes by both black and white Populist leaders. However, these gains should not be exaggerated, for even within the increased democracy of Populist politics, the Negro still had to adjust himself to less than full equality. The Populist would often speak out for political equality for the Negro, but never social equality. White Populists made this dis-tinction and Negro Populists had to accommodate them-selves. Negro Populists were in what amounted to a parallel organisation. There were Negro Populist clubs and picnics, barbecues and camp meetings for black Populists. Both races were welcomed at party speeches and rallies—blacks to one side, whites to the other.

Segregation and Disfranchisement[7]

The *entente* with the white Populists was but a brief flash

[7] For the best and most succinct account of the movement toward segregation and disfranchisement, cf. C. Vann Woodward, *The Strange Career of Jim Crow.*

of light in what was to become an increasingly dark period
for the Negro in the South. Radical Reconstruction had
left the South unreconstructed. The North had won the war,
but lost the peace. By 1877 Federal troops had been with-
drawn from the South and government restored to the hands
of the Southern whites. The exigencies of political compromise and a general loss of faith in the crusade for the
Negro on the part of the North had brought this about.
This did not immediately bring about the re-establishment
of white supremacy—that would come with time. Negroes
did continue to vote in the South for a while, but in de-
creased numbers.

Gradually through the erection of an elaborate legal
structure, the Southern states sought to assign the Negro to
his 'proper place'. Segregation in certain areas of Southern
life was made mandatory. This movement first concentrated
on segregation of public transport—streetcars and railroads
—but continued with increased impetus and widening scope
during the period of wholesale reversion to white supremacy
in the 1890s. By the time Oklahoma came into the Union
in 1907 segregation was the accepted legal practice throughout the South, being required in waiting rooms, theatres,
boarding-houses, water fountains, ticket windows, peni-
tentiaries, county jails, convict camps, institutions for the
deaf and blind, mental hospitals and, of course, state-run
schools.[8]

The movement toward segregation was aided and
abetted both by the general temper of the times and by an
increasingly restrictive interpretation of the Fourteenth
Amendment (equal protection of the laws) by the U.S.
Supreme Court. Imperialism was at its zenith in the last
years of the nineteenth century; Europe was tramping
through Asia and Africa, and the idea of the 'white man's
burden' gained general acceptance among white men
everywhere. If it was reasonable for white men to go into

[8] United States Commission on Civil Rights, *Freedom to the Free:
1863–1963 Century of Emancipation*, pp. 60–61.

'backward areas' in distant parts of the world and have
dominion over the darker peoples there, 'why should not
the same be true for white men in the South?' asked those
who wished to relegate the Negro to an inferior position in
American life. The North was in no mood to give a rebuttal.
Indeed, it usually acquiesced in or encouraged this view.
The attitude was summed up by the editor of the *Atlantic
Monthly*, supposedly one of the nation's more 'enlightened'
magazines:

If the stronger and cleverer race is free to impose its will upon
'new-caught sullen peoples' on the other side of the globe,
why not in South Carolina and Mississippi?[9]

The narrow interpretation by the Supreme Court of the
Fourteenth Amendment in the latter part of the nineteenth
century dashed to the ground the dreams of all those who,
after the Civil War, had seen in the adoption of this amendment new hope for the establishment of true equality before
the law in the United States. In the *Civil Rights Cases* (1883),
the Court held that the Fourteenth Amendment prohibited
states from discriminating against citizens on the ground of
colour, but that it did *not* restrict private individuals or
organisations from doing so. This gave legal sanction to the
practice of segregation on railroads, in hotels, theatres and
similar places. The high-water mark in this move toward
the entrenchment of segregation, however, was not reached
until 1896 when in the now famous *Plessy* v. *Ferguson* case
the Court upheld state legislation that discriminated against
Negroes, saying that separation of accommodations did not
deprive the Negro of equal rights as long as the accommodations were equal. The doctrine of 'Separate, but Equal'
provided the South with a veil—however thin—with which
to cloak their discriminatory practices for years to come.

Although the introduction of Jim Crow laws began on a
wide scale soon after the white Southerners had been
returned to power, the move for disfranchisement of the

[9] Quoted in Vann Woodward, *op. cit.*, p. 70.

Negro did not reach full strength until the 1890s. The *entente* for political purposes between certain black and white agrarian elements in the South had frightened many whites. In the days immediately following restoration of white rule, a rich new breed of industrialists or would-be industrialists, known as Bourbons or Redeemers, had taken over and maintained power by manipulation of the Negro vote as a bloc. When white Populists during the period of agrarian unrest began to form alliances with the black farmers, a situation arose in which the whites were often fighting among themselves for the Negro vote, which meant that the Negro often held the balance of power. This was a situation the whites were bound to find intolerable. The Redeemers and the white agrarian element alike decided that it was time white men closed ranks and eliminated the Negro as a political factor altogether. This would make political problems for both white groups less complicated and would placate the masses of the Southern white populace who had been against the idea of Negro suffrage all along. Through the 1890s and on into the early part of the twentieth century individual Southern states devised laws and other ways of separating the Negro from his vote, making it appear that this was not done on the basis of race since to do so would have been in contravention of the Fifteenth Amendment. Among the devices employed were the poll tax, special property-owning qualifications and literacy and understanding tests. The latter required the prospective voter to read and interpret a part of the Constitution in order to qualify to vote. The judgement as to the 'correctness' of the interpretation lay in the hands of the local registrar.

These methods served their purpose quite well, but it often turned out that poor white men were also being disfranchised by them. In response to their protests, many states adopted 'grandfather clauses' in their state voting laws. These made it possible for men who could not meet the literacy and property qualifications to be admitted to the franchise if their ancestors had voted before 1867 or some date before Reconstruction began.[10]

John Mercer Langston, the only Negro ever elected to Congress (House of Representatives) from Virginia, Frederick Douglass, until his death in 1895, and other individual Negroes in positions of responsibility, continually raised their voices in protest throughout this period—but all to no avail. There were too few who wished to listen. For the time being at least, the South was to have its own way in the establishment and protection of its 'way of life'.

Du Bois, The Niagara Movement and Mr. Washington

Events in the year 1895 further darkened an already dark time in the history of Negro protest in America. In that year the fiery protest leader Frederick Douglass died, and the Virginia-born ex-slave, Booker T. Washington, made his famous 'Atlanta Compromise' speech before the Cotton States' Exposition. This speech catapulted him into an unprecedentedly strong position of Negro leadership. Seemingly, Washington by advocating a de-emphasis of civil rights for Negroes and repudiating social equality had told white America exactly what it wanted to hear. Whites rushed to support Washington and his programme for increased industrial education for the Negro. He was declared a 'Negro leader' and regarded as the spokesman for the Negro race. Washington achieved a position of remarkable strength in the affairs of the Negro in America and of immense power in the influencing of public opinion.[11] Apparently, Washington did hope for eventual social justice but believed that accommodation and not protest was the order of the day.

[10] T. Harry Williams, Richard N. Current, and Frank Freidel, *A History of the United States*, vol. 1, New York, 1959, pp. 672–674.
[11] Samuel R. Spencer, Jr., *Booker T. Washington and the Negro's Place in American Life*, pp. 162–177. Spencer calls Washington a 'benevolent despot'. He points to the arbitrary power Washington had over the allocation of large sums from Northern foundations and the control he exercised over the Negro press, including his secret ownership of the *New York Age*, the largest Negro newspaper in America.

However, the accommodationist leadership of Booker T. Washington was not to go unchallenged. The voice of Negro protest was born again on the lips of a group of militant Negro intellectuals who repudiated the fallacy that Washington spoke for all Negroes.[12] Among these men were Monroe Trotter, spirited editor of the *Boston Guardian*, John Hope, President of Atlanta Baptist College and, by far the most outstanding, Dr. William E. B. Du Bois. Du Bois, a Massachusetts-born, Harvard and European-trained scholar, stepped to the very head of the attack on Washington's position and remained there for decades to follow. Du Bois pressed vigorously for equal rights and attacked the Washington concept of industrial education for the Negro. It was Du Bois' view that:

. . . the final product of our training must be neither a psychologist nor a brickmason, but a man. And to make men, we must have ideals, broad, pure, and inspiring ends of living . . .[13]

In the summer of 1905, Du Bois and twenty-eight other Negro intellectuals met at Niagara Falls, Canada in the hope of forming a national protest organisation.[14] The group advocated an organised and aggressive defence of Negro civil rights throughout the country. The Niagara Movement met twice more, but never attained any great strength. It was nevertheless important in that it reflected a growing differentiation within the Negro community itself. Throughout slavery and the years immediately following, the overwhelming majority of American Negroes shared a common lot. With emancipation and the growth of an educated class, the spectrum of opinion and personal situation widened, and it became more difficult to speak of 'the Negro leader' or of 'the Negro community' that he

[12] Daniel Walder, 'The Contemporary Opposition to the Political and Educational Ideals of Booker T. Washington'.
[13] W. E. B. Du Bois, *The Souls of Black Folk*, p. 72.
[14] They met on the Canadian side since the conference met discrimination in the Buffalo hotel at which it had reservations.

purported to represent. With the advent of the Niagara Movement, we have for the first time a genuine Negro intelligentsia organising on a national scale to draw up protests and to work for social change. The Movement is significant in that it provided alternatives to the monocracy of Booker T. Washington, and in that it was to be a forerunner of the modern National Association for the Advancement of Colored People.

Early Days of the N.A.A.C.P.

The National Association for the Advancement of Colored People grew out of a conference held in 1909 to protest against the vicious Springfield race riot of the summer of the previous year.[15] The 'young radicals' of the Niagara Movement were invited to the conference, which had been initiated by Mary White Ovington, Oswald Garrison Villard and other white liberals. Plans were made at this conference for the establishment of a permanent organisation that would work for 'the abolition of all forced segregation, equal education for Negro and white children, the complete enfranchisement of the Negro, and the enforcement of the Fourteenth and Fifteenth Amendments'.[16]

A legal redress committee was formed soon after the founding of the N.A.A.C.P. and some important legal victories were won in the earliest days of the organisation—beginning with the Supreme Court decision against the 'grandfather clauses' in 1915. Research and public information, another phase of the Association's programme, was under the direction of Dr. DuBois. By 1921, the N.A.A.C.P. had more than 400 branches throughout the country and was well on its way to long years of service in the cause of integration in America.

The alliance of the white liberals with the Negro leaders in the formation of the N.A.A.C.P. was in the old abolitionist

[15] James Crouthamel, 'The Springfield Race Riot of 1908', *The Journal of Negro History*, XLV, July 1960, pp. 164–181.
[16] John Hope Franklin, *From Slavery to Freedom*, p. 439.

tradition. This form of protest was significantly new, however, in that it was national in character, had the benefit
of Negro intellectuals, and was equipped for a modern legal
and public information programme. The N.A.A.C.P. was
the first national protest organisation of its kind.

The Garvey Movement

Amid the shock and disillusionment following the First
World War there arose yet another form of Negro protest—
the black nationalism of the Garvey movement. This was
the first and up to now the greatest mass movement among
American Negroes. Marcus M. Garvey was a Jamaican
endowed with a vision of black unity and a faith that he
would be the main instrument in effecting that unity.

His programme was a type of black Zionism. Garvey
wished to build a state in Africa to which Negroes from all
over the world could come and live. Garvey was the first
leader to teach the Negro masses to be proud that they were
black. He gave them a new sense of meaning, an awareness
of self and a proud identity. His black nationalism revelled
in racial glorification and race history. His programme
called for independence from the white man and economic
self-sufficiency. His charge to the nation's and the world's
coloured masses was, 'Up you mighty race, you can accom-
plish what you will'. Garvey claimed some 2 million
members in his Universal Negro Improvement Association
(U.N.I.A.).[17] Though this figure may be inflated, it is true
that Garvey owned the allegiance of Negroes in all parts of
the world, especially among the masses of the United States
where he had carried out most of his work.

Many of Garvey's business ventures failed or embroiled
him in legal tangles. Finally, he was arrested and deported
by the Federal Government in 1927 on charges of using the
mails to defraud in connexion with his Black Star steamship
line. The conviction grew more out of pressure within the

[17] Edmund D. Cronon, *Black Moses: The Story of Marcus Garvey and the
Universal Negro Improvement Association*, p. 44.

nation to get rid of Garvey and Garvey's own business ineptitude than out of any conscious malfeasance on his part. At any rate, deprived of Garvey's charisma the movement rapidly deteriorated. However, the masses were not soon to forget Garvey and even today his name is spoken with a certain sainted reverence by black nationalists throughout America.

Myrdal captures well the significance of the birth of this form of protest movement, when he says of Garvey and the U.N.I.A.:

For one thing, it proves that it *is* possible to reach the Negro masses if they are appealed to in an effective way. It testifies to the basic unrest in the Negro community. It tells of a dissatisfaction so deep that it mounts to hopelessness of ever gaining a full life in America.[18]

Remnants of the Garvey movement continued to function throughout the thirties. The N.A.A.C.P. level of activity was relatively high then as it continued to push its campaign for anti-lynching legislation, fair administration of justice, Negro voting rights in the South, elimination of discrimination from industry and equal opportunity in education. On the whole, however, there was very little that was new in the way of constructive organised civil rights protest. The Negro was too involved in the business of finding his daily bread and simply keeping alive in this difficult period. The Great Depression made almost all Americans pull their belts a little tighter, but for the American Negro who was already used to a tight belt over a taut stomach it was a particularly hard time. The utter frustration felt by the masses of urban Negroes in the North often found its outlet and expression in new off-beat escapist cults such as the Father Divine 'bread and peace' movement[19] or the Black Muslims in their earliest days.[20] The discontent sometimes erupted more violently in riots in some of the nation's black ghettos.

---

[18] Myrdal, *op. cit.*, p. 749.
[19] See Roi Otterly, *New World A-Coming*, Boston, 1943.
[20] See Chapter IV, below.

March on Washington

The coming of the Second World War brought economic change, and with it new impetus for Negro protest. The Negro wanted assurance that the full exercise of the rights he was fighting to defend would be granted to him. The N.A.A.C.P. and other protest groups were quick to point out the incongruities in a man's offering his life to preserve privileges for his countrymen which he himself did not yet possess. New, organised Negro protest that came out of the war was to redound to both the Negro's immediate good and to his long-range benefit in the post-war years.

The greatest and most significant protest to come out of the war, both in terms of what it taught the nation about the Negro's dissatisfaction, and what it taught the Negro about the nature of effective protest, was the March on Washington Movement, initiated by A. Philip Randolph, the organiser of the Brotherhood of Sleeping Car Porters.

The grievance centred around the fact that many war plants with government contracts refused to employ Negro workers. Randolph sent out a challenge to the Negroes of America: 'Let us march 10,000 strong on Washington, D.C. Only force can effect enforcement, and Negroes are getting nowhere in national defense. The whole national set-up reeks and stinks with race prejudice, hatred, and discrimination.'[21] Large delegations of Negroes from all over the country prepared to march on the capital on 1 June 1941. The march was held in temporary abeyance while President Roosevelt had a conference with Randolph and other Negro leaders. The Negroes would not be daunted. Finally, on 25 June 1941, President Roosevelt issued Executive Order 8802, prohibiting discrimination in industries holding government contracts and establishing a Committee on Fair Employment Practices.

[21] A. Philip Randolph, 'The Most Dangerous Negro in America', *Negro Digest*, September 1961, p. 7. From Arna Bontemps, *100 Years of Negro Freedom*, New York, 1961.

The protest had worked, and from its success the Negro had been given a new estimation of his power to effect social change. The success of the March on Washington Movement gave the Negro one of the first hints of the power of non-violent direct-action protest. The type of non-violent direct action and personal involvement which the Negroes had been prepared to employ on a large scale represented a new approach to Negro protest.

The years following the Second World War found the Negro trying many methods in his quest for full freedom. Some of these methods were new and different in form, others quite conventional and familiar. It is to the history of three different forms of Negro protest since the war and the way in which they are related to each other and to the larger historical picture that we now turn.

II. THROUGH THE COURTS OF JUSTICE

Our Constitution is color-blind, and neither knows nor tolerates classes among citizens. In respect of civil rights, all citizens are equal before the law. The humblest is the peer of the most powerful . . .

Justice HARLAN, dissenting in *Plessy* v. *Ferguson* (1896).

Hence we call upon all the believers in democracy to join in a national conference for the discussion of present evils, the voicing of protests, and the renewal of the struggle for civil and political liberty.

OSWALD GARRISON VILLARD in *The Call*, originating the conference from which the N.A.A.C.P. was born (1909).

We conclude that in the field of public education the doctrine of 'separate but equal' has no place. Separate educational facilities are inherently unequal.

Chief Justice EARL WARREN in the Public School Desegregation Cases, 17 May 1954.

The National Association for the Advancement of Colored People and the Traditional Approach

SINCE its birth in 1909, the National Association for the Advancement of Colored People has sought 'to end racial discrimination in all public aspects of American life'. However, the organisation as it exists today is quite different from the N.A.A.C.P. of the days of Villard and Du Bois. Called 'radical' at its foundation (as indeed it was for those times), the N.A.A.C.P. has grown from the militant protest organisation of a small number of intellectuals into a large nation-wide association with an elaborate bureaucracy. Over the years, this 'radical' organisation has also achieved a certain degree of acceptance and middle-class respectability. Protest has been institutionalised and the general public has become accustomed to having the N.A.A.C.P. around in much the same way that it has accepted the interest group organisations of labourers, farmers and manufacturers. This development from small unstructured protest of specific grievances to the large, institutionalised, bureaucratic approach is typical of the history of many pressure groups in the U.S.A.—of labour for example.[1]

The methods used by the N.A.A.C.P. to bring about change are also fairly typical. The emphasis is on the legal approach and public education; the roles of the lawyer and the public relations man are paramount. The N.A.A.C.P. and other groups like it that are seeking social reform operate on the assumption that an informed public and the traditional channels of judicial appeal are all that are necessary to bring about the desired social change. It is in this sense that the N.A.A.C.P. protest is typically 'American'.

It has been the upper-class and educated Negro who has exercised the dominant influence in the organisation over the years—this largely due to the sophisticated nature of N.A.A.C.P. protest and the necessity of having trained and intelligent men to carry out the legal and educational programme. However, the N.A.A.C.P. is regarded as speaking for and representing *all* Negroes, and is anxious to maintain this hegemony, in the face of any challenge.

The N.A.A.C.P. operates today as a highly mechanised and hierarchic organisation.[2] It continues to exhibit its faith in the conventional channels of change by its extensive legal and public educational programmes. The Association currently claims a membership of more than 370,000 persons in forty-four states and the District of Columbia. There are 1,200 local branches of the N.A.A.C.P.[2]

The Organisation and Operation of the N.A.A.C.P.

Broadly speaking, there are three levels of organisation in the N.A.A.C.P.—national, regional and local. The basic policies of the Association are developed at its annual conventions by delegates representing the local N.A.A.C.P. units. The control and governing of the N.A.A.C.P. is the responsibility of a forty-eight member Board of Directors,

[1] For a discussion of a parallel development from localised protest to institutionalised bureaucracy, see F. R. Dulles, *Labor in America*, New York, 1949.
[2] *This is the N.A.A.C.P.*, p. 1.

elected by the branches, which meets every month at the national headquarters located on West 40th Street in New York City. The policies of the convention and the Board are carried out by an employed staff, headed by the Executive Secretary, who is chosen by the Board. The current Executive Secretary, Roy Wilkins, has served in that position since 1955 when he succeeded Walter White. White had been Executive Secretary for twenty-four years at the time of his death.

The various departments of the national organisation operate under the supervision of the Executive Secretary. The Public Relations Department fulfils the very important function of explaining the organisation to the general public. The director of this department publicises the current achievements of the Association and serves as an information source for those wishing to learn about race relations. This department is also responsible for keeping the administrative heads apprised of public reaction to N.A.A.C.P. policies.[3] A sub-division of the Public Relations Department is the Division of Information and Research, established in 1942. This division is especially concerned with providing information and guidance to ' schools, libraries, race relations committees, civic bodies, and other groups and individuals interested in advancing democratic concepts and furthering racial understanding'.[4]

In addition to the Public Relations Department, there is the Department of Special Research, set up in 1944. This handles various specific research projects and, in general, collects important facts pertaining to Negro life in America and throughout the world. Its director often represents the N.A.A.C.P. at college forums and lectures to special organisations.

The Department of Branches is yet another of the important subsidiary units of the national association. It

[3] Warren D. St. James, *The National Association for the Advancement of Colored People: A Case Study in Pressure Groups*, p. 64.
[4] *Ibid.*

derives a great deal of its importance from the responsibility it has for co-ordinating the programme of the local branches, youth councils and college chapters. It has been correctly pointed out that, 'the strength and influence of the N.A.A.C.P. lies in the well-organised local branches at grass-roots level'.[5] Apart from its great judicial victories, the N.A.A.C.P. has experienced its greatest success in the specific campaigns of well-organised local units attacking some form of discrimination or segregation in their communities or areas.

The Washington Bureau of the Association fulfils very necessary functions for the organisation. The bureau is in charge of analysing bills pending in Congress that might somehow relate to the Negro's situation. After study, it is decided whether the N.A.A.C.P. will support or oppose the proposed legislation. The bureau compiles voting records of senators and representatives and informs the local branches of the stands taken by their Congressmen. It also makes tabulations showing the majority by which a Congressman has been elected and then juxtaposes these figures with the number of Negroes of voting age in the state or district. The director of the bureau keeps in contact with congressional leaders and the heads of federal agencies. He often appears before congressional committees to support or oppose prospective legislation.

Early in 1947, the N.A.A.C.P. established its Church Department. Its job is to co-ordinate the activities of religious groups with the N.A.A.C.P. in its struggle for integration. The Association recognises the great numerical strength and influence of the church in the Negro community and, although leading churchmen have always co-operated with it and churches have often been the main meeting places for conventions and mass meetings, the N.A.A.C.P. still feels that there is a wealth of untapped resources in the Negro church. This concern with the churches also indicates that the N.A.A.C.P. recognises them as a potential threat to its own dominance. Although the

[5] St. James, *op. cit.*, p. 65.

formation of the Church Department took place before the
Rev. Martin Luther King and the Montgomery bus boycott,
the N.A.A.C.P. had already realised that an alternative to
its leadership might come from among clergymen and the
organised churches. In a case such as this the standard practice of the N.A.A.C.P. is simply to widen its sphere of
influence, engulfing its prospective challenger to the point
that it becomes identified with N.A.A.C.P. leadership. This
process was even tried with the sit-ins. Though N.A.A.C.P.
officials were forced to admit that they would have dis-
couraged the sit-in protests had the students come to them
first, after the blossoming of the current movement the
N.A.A.C.P. was anxious to be identified with it and its
success. It was quick to point out that the current sit-in
movement, generally taken to have begun in February
1960, actually started two years earlier with the sit-ins of
one of its youth branches in Oklahoma City, so that, after
all, the N.A.A.C.P. had really been the originator of the
sit-ins.[6]

The director of the Church Department travels widely,
making contacts with churches of all denominations, and
trying to secure the participation of their members in the
work of the N.A.A.C.P. branches in their respective
communities. The director often speaks at large church
conferences, encouraging aggressive church participation
in the Association's membership drive and programme. It is
also true that 'in many rural areas the interwoven programmes of the church and N.A.A.C.P. provide the main
basis for the existence of N.A.A.C.P. branches'.[7]

[6] Roy Wilkins, Executive Secretary of the N.A.A.C.P. in a speech before
the City Club Forum of Cleveland, Ohio on 16 April 1960. Published
by the N.A.A.C.P. under the title, 'The Meaning of the Sit-Ins', September 1960. N.A.A.C.P. counsel, Constance B. Motley was quick to point
out the Oklahoma sit-in to me, at the beginning of a personal interview
I had with her. The N.A.A.C.P. has also reprinted an article on the
Oklahoma City sit-in for the 1960 *Datebook Magazine*, entitled, 'Why I
Sit In', by Barbara Ann Posey.
[7] St. James, *op. cit.*, p. 66.

Owing to the nature of the N.A.A.C.P. programme, the legal department is of central importance to the organisation. It is in the area of legal battles that the N.A.A.C.P. has made its most significant advances throughout its history. In recent years it has won almost every Supreme Court case in which it has been involved. Since 1941, N.A.A.C.P. lawyers have successfully argued 43 of the 47 cases in which they have appeared before the Supreme Court.[8] Officially, the legal arm of the Association is really a separate organisation—the N.A.A.C.P. Legal Defense and Educational Fund. It was incorporated as an autonomous legal aid society in 1940 in order that it might maintain its tax-exempt status, as it could not do as part of a national organisation with a Washington lobby. The legal defence organisation handles or supervises cases involving coloured persons when their equal protection under the law may be in doubt. Cases are brought to it by local branches, the national organisation and by other civil rights groups.[9]

Below the national organisation are the various forms of local organisation: regional offices; state conferences; and branches, including youth councils and college chapters. There are three regional offices: one in Atlanta for the south-east, one in Dallas for the south-west, and one in San Francisco for the West Coast. These offices act as connecting links between the national office and the branches. There are also regional conferences held every year to plan programme and policy and to train and guide branch leadership. In several states, there are state conferences which try to stimulate branch activity within the state and organise new branches. There are also seven N.A.A.C.P. field secretaries who travel around the country conducting campaigns, reorganising branches and setting up new units.

The work of the Association relies heavily upon the effectiveness of its branches. A local branch is chartered

[8] United States Civil Rights Commission, *op. cit.*, p. 162.
[9] The N.A.A.C.P. Legal Defense and Educational Fund is currently handling many of the Freedom Ride cases for the Congress of Racial Equality.

upon application to the Board of Directors by fifty or more persons living in a locality. The Youth Councils in local communities operate under the adult branches, and the college chapters have a total membership of approximately 6,000 in colleges throughout the country. Myrdal has summarised succinctly the role of the branches, a summary which is indicative of the importance of the grass-root activities to the organisation as a whole:

The branches are to assume responsibility for the general welfare of the Negro population of the particular locality. In carrying out the broad program enunciated by the National Office, they are local vigilant groups covering all of the ramifications of Negro life in a prejudice ridden milieu. The Branches are to check on 'biased and discriminatory administration of the law, and injustice in the courts.' They are to combat attempts at racial discrimination in civil rights, parks, museums, theaters, conveyances and other public places, and in charitable and public agencies. They are expected to bring test cases on the rights of Negro citizens before the courts, where great injustice is done because of race or color prejudice.[10]

No small task for any organisation.

The Association has as its official organ *The Crisis*, a monthly magazine which gives information about the activities of the N.A.A.C.P. and on race relations in America in general.

Through this complicated organisational set-up, the N.A.A.C.P. works to remove the barriers of discrimination and segregation. It exerts its pressure in three basic areas: the public, through its information and education programme; the courts of justice at local, state and federal levels; and among legislators and public administrators, at all levels of their activity.

Achievements

Except in instances of major court victories in which the N.A.A.C.P. has been directly involved and in the successes

[10] Myrdal, *op. cit.*, p. 822.

of specific projects effected by local N.A.A.C.P. branches throughout the country, it is difficult to catalogue the recent achievements of the organisation. This is because laws and changes in public policy often come about through a complex of forces, and cannot be attributed *exclusively* to the N.A.A.C.P., even when the organisation has obviously had some part in bringing about the change. Thus the diminution of lynching or the passage of a Civil Rights Act cannot really be called N.A.A.C.P. 'victories' although it has waged a vigorous anti-lynching campaign for over fifty years and has continually lobbied Congress for a Civil Rights Act. At least, they cannot be called N.A.A.C.P. 'victories' in the same sense that the 1954 Supreme Court decision on school segregation can; or the hiring of Negro bus drivers in Dallas, or the opening of hospitals in Wheeling after specific projects of the local branch organisation.

The N.A.A.C.P. has played a crucial role in bringing about a betterment of racial conditions in America both tangibly, as reflected in changes of public policy and intangibly, as reflected by changes in public attitudes and awareness. Among these advances we might include the enactment by 1960 of fair housing laws in fourteen states, and the passage of Fair Employment Practices laws in fifteen states and forty cities.[11] President Truman's Executive Order, banning discrimination in the armed forces came about as a result of pressure from the N.A.A.C.P. and other groups.

In the courts the N.A.A.C.P. has handled and won most of the recent Supreme Court cases dealing with discrimination and segregation. It has brought about the abolition of judicial enforcement of racially restrictive covenants in housing. It has brought about the invalidation of state

[11] Figures cited by Whitney Young, Executive Director of the Urban League in a speech at the International Students Association, Cambridge, Massachusetts, 7 March 1961.

statutes requiring racial segregation in education, transportation and recreation.[12]

Through its programme of information and education,
the N.A.A.C.P. has brought about greater recognition of
Negro achievement. The Association is responsible in many
ways for a more favourable image of the Negro in the media
of mass communication, and has helped to destroy the Negro
stereotype. It has also given the Negro a greater awareness
of his political strength. Negroes, it has been shown, played
a decisive role in the Presidential election of 1960; the white
vote was about evenly divided between the two candidates,
while Negroes voted 70 per cent in favour of Kennedy.

By far, the greatest of N.A.A.C.P. triumphs in recent years
was the Supreme Court decision in the five public school
segregation cases of 17 May 1954. The court held that 'in
the field of public education the doctrine of "separate but
equal" has no place'. The fifty-eight year old doctrine of
Plessy v. *Ferguson* was dead, and a whole new era of American
social history began. The 1954 decision was the result of
years of hard work and planning. Over the years the
Association had increasingly won cases in the field of
education in their insistence on a strict interpretation of the
'equal' in the court's old 'separate but equal' doctrine.
'Equal' came to mean more than just tangible facilities,
and the court was finally to decide that it was impossible to
have separate but equal facilities in public (state) schools.
The implications of this decision for the future of the
American social system are great. It seems to portend the
end of all forms of segregation in public life. The N.A.A.C.P.
has followed this decision up with great vigour, not intend-
ing to let school integration remain only a 'paper right'.
It was through the N.A.A.C.P.'s efforts that James H.
Meredith was admitted to the formerly impregnable

[12] *Morgan* v. *Commonwealth of Virginia*, 328 U.S. 373, was a major breakthrough, prohibiting segregation in interstate travel (1946). Subsequent
victories have been won in various cases dealing with public facilities,
and in the area of education the historic Brown decision of 17 May 1954
was the most momentous of all.

University of Mississippi in the fall of 1962. Constance Baker
Motley, counsel for the N.A.A.C.P., also feels that the
decision has further significance owing to the role it has had
in stimulating a new awareness and militancy on the part of
the Negro in his struggle for his constitutional rights. She sees
the whole direct-action non-violence movement as being
intimately bound up in its genesis with the 17 May decision.
In commenting on it, Mrs. Motley said, 'To the man in the
street, the court has said, "Negroes are just as good as
anyone else"' and now they are taking a more active part to
make sure they are *treated* the same as anyone else.

Opposition to the N.A.A.C.P.

The recent successes of the N.A.A.C.P. have certainly not
gone unnoticed by whites who feel menaced by the advances
the Association is making in the field of integration. Shortly
after the 1954 decision the National Association for the
Advancement of White People was founded. Throughout
the South, White Citizens' Councils were formed, and there
were reports of the revival of the Ku Klux Klan. Although
the N.A.A.C.P. often meets criticism from various sources
for being too 'conservative', it is this organisation that the
white South apparently sees as most threatening—at least
judging from the elaborate legal impediments imposed
upon its operation by Southern states. The action of
Southern states in their programme to oppose the N.A.A.C.P.
has alarmed many people interested in civil liberties, who
see the devices as a danger not only to the N.A.A.C.P., but
to the freedom of association and the right of protest in the
South.

Methods that have been employed, or at least attempted,
include:[13]

1. Discriminatory use of existing laws to halt the organisation's activity. Alabama, Georgia, Louisiana and Texas

[13] The various methods are described in a publication of the American
Jewish Congress, Benjamin Mintz, Richard Spenser and Joseph B.
Robison, *Assault Upon Freedom of Association*, pp. 31–35.

have tried to curb the N.A.A.C.P. by accusing it of failure
to comply with existing state laws. In Texas and Georgia
it was claimed that the Association was in fact making a
profit and therefore was not entitled to tax exemption as a
non-profit organisation. This has been used as an excuse for
seizing records and demanding membership lists.   In
Alabama in 1956 the Association was charged with failure
to register as an out-of-state corporation and to provide the
state with information required by Alabama law. In
Louisiana it was charged with violation of a 1924 state law
that required the officers of every 'fraternal, patriotic,
charitable, benevolent, literary, scientific, athletic, military,
or social organization, or organizations created for similar
purposes, whether incorporated or unincorporated', to file
yearly membership lists with the Louisiana Secretary of
State.[14] The law had never before been invoked, except
against the Ku Klux Klan.

2. Bans on state employees' membership in specified
organisations. Until it was challenged in the courts, South
Carolina had a law which provided that no state employee
could belong to the N.A.A.C.P. Georgia first directed
revocation of the licence of any Georgia teacher who
belonged to the N.A.A.C.P., and then achieved the same
end by holding that membership in the N.A.A.C.P. was
inconsistent with the oath to defend the constitution and
laws of the state which all state employees must take. In
1956 Louisiana passed a series of laws prohibiting school
employees from doing anything that promoted integration.
(A subsequent Supreme Court decision struck down these
statutes in part.) Mississippi has required school employees
to reveal their affiliations with any organisation, with a
threat of action against N.A.A.C.P. members implied.

3. Publication of membership lists. Devices for exposure
of membership of the Association have been employed in
states throughout the South, through court proceedings,

[14] Mintz, Spenser and Robison, *op. cit.*, p. 17.

through frankly discriminatory legislation or by demand of legislative investigating committees.

4. Requiring registration. Registration statutes often have other ways of hindering and over-burdening an organisation; the law in Arkansas, for example, requires pro-integration groups to have receipted bills of all expenditure regardless of how small, giving the name and address of the person who receive the money. Compliance with such a law requires an extraordinary amount of energy simply in keeping records.

5. Special taxation. Only in Alabama, in one county, has this technique been used against the N.A.A.C.P. In rural Wilcox County where the Negro population is relatively high, a bill passed in 1955 requires all organisations soliciting money in the county to pay a $200 licence fee, $50 for each solicitor and $5 for each person enrolling in the organisation. The bill's sponsor, Representative Sam Nettles, made clear his intentions for the bill. He said, 'Without such a proposal, it would be very easy for the N.A.A.C.P. to slip into Wilcox County and teach the Negroes undesirable ideas.'[15]

6. Anti-barratry laws. These laws passed in Georgia, Mississippi, South Carolina, Tennessee and Virginia prohibit support of lawsuits by persons or organisations not having direct interest in them. These statutes were passed with the N.A.A.C.P. in mind, but they make it difficult to challenge any law the state legislature may choose to pass.

7. Legislative investigations. State legislative investigating committees have used their broad general powers to harass and to enquire into the activities of the N.A.A.C.P., which has been the subject of hearings in Florida, Louisiana and Virginia.

8. Emergency powers. Florida and Georgia have 'emergency' legislation provisions which impose virtually no limit upon the state's powers. The Governor may declare an

[15] Mintz, Spenser and Robison, *op. cit.*, p. 11.

'emergency' at his own discretion. He may then stop organisational activity as a threat to the 'peace and good order of
society'.

Part of the attack on the N.A.A.C.P. has been in the form
of slur campaigns, charging the organisation with Communist activities. White supremacists all over the South
openly allege that the N.A.A.C.P. is 'Communist-domin-
ated' and 'subversive'. Attorney-General Eugene Cook of
Georgia stated that he had proof that the N.A.A.C.P. is a
'front and tool' of subversive groups in the United States—
evidence he has somehow never produced.[16] The N.A.A.C.P.
has always been clear, unequivocal and explicit in opposition
to Communism. This fact did not escape several important
Southern newspapers which, during the height of the smear
campaign, felt compelled to point out that though the
N.A.A.C.P. was unpopular, it was simply not true that
it was a Communist or Communist-inspired organisation.
J. Edgar Hoover, who has denounced the frequent 'Communist' charge made against the N.A.A.C.P., is often cited
in this connexion. In the keynote address before the Association's Fortieth Annual Convention in 1949, Roy Wilkins
summed up the Americanism of the Negro and the
N.A.A.C.P.   He said :

In demanding these things [civil rights] . . . we do not cry out
bitterly that we love another land better than our own, or another
people better than ours.

This is our land. This is our nation. We helped build it. We
have defended it from Boston Common to Iwo Jima. . . . we are
Americans, and in the American way, with American weapons,
and with American determination to be free, we intend to . . .
fight right here on this home front if it takes forty more summers—
until victory is ours.[17]

Organised opposition of these kinds has certainly ham-
pered the operation of the N.A.A.C.P. in the South, but

[16] Attorney-General Eugene Cook, quoted in *N.A.A.C.P.—An American
Organisation*, p. 11.
[17] *Ibid.*, p. 12.

has not stopped it. The validity of many of the obstructionist measures imposed by the states is being challenged and the N.A.A.C.P. has already received favourable rulings in some instances.[18]

Criticisms of the N.A.A.C.P.

One of the major charges levelled against the N.A.A.C.P. with increasing frequency in recent years is its remoteness from the Negro masses it seeks to represent. Many of the more militant integrationists see the N.A.A.C.P. as being too 'middle-class' and 'conservative'. Black nationalist leaders in the leading metropolitan areas often berate the organisation and its absence from among the lower-class Negroes. 'Leaders who don't live with us, can't think for us', is often the cry. In recent years membership of the N.A.A.C.P. has declined, and the decline has been particularly noticeable in the large urban areas where the lower class Negroes live. It declined by 15,000 in 1961 alone. Herbert Hill, labour secretary of the N.A.A.C.P., points out that this is at least partly attributable to the disproportionately high number of Negro workers unemployed in 1961 who were unable to pay dues ($2 a year). But this explanation is partial at best. It fails to take into account the great and growing feeling of militancy in the Negro community, which has decided that the N.A.A.C.P. is not vigorous enough in its programme for equal rights for the

[18] On 15 December 1960 the Supreme Court gave a favourable ruling to the N.A.A.C.P. in declaring invalid an Arkansas law requiring public school teachers to list their organisational affiliations. A $100,000 fining of the N.A.A.C.P. by the State of Alabama was set aside by the Supreme Court in 1958. On 28 December 1962 a Virginia Circuit Court ruled unconstitutional a state law which would have opened N.A.A.C.P. membership lists. And on 25 March 1963 the U.S. Supreme Court in a very far-reaching and important decision barred legislative investigators from enquiring into the membership of organisations which are 'neither engaged in subversive or other illegal or improper activities, nor demonstrated to have any substantial connexions with such activities'. The case arose out of the conviction of a former President of the Miami branch of the N.A.A.C.P. for refusing to produce a membership list to a Florida legislature committee investigating possible Communist infiltration of the N.A.A.C.P.

black man. Dissatisfaction and disillusionment with the current rate of 'progress' and conventional methods of protest has gripped many. Many are beginning to feel like the Negro resident of Birmingham, Alabama who told the N.A.A.C.P. representative who was investigating the drop in membership in that city, 'Here's my $2. Take it and do what you want with it. But keep your membership. I have got my gun now'.[17]

Historically, it is true that the N.A.A.C.P. has been largely what might be called a 'middle-class' organisation. It has always drawn heavily on the Negro intelligentsia for its membership. This is still true today. But this does not mean that the N.A.A.C.P. is not alive to the needs of the majority of the nation's Negroes. Far from it. Its wide range of legal, legislative and educational programmes all serve the betterment of American Negroes at any level of society—and probably most often those in the lower socio-economic bracket. The deficiency of the N.A.A.C.P. does not seem to be that it is not doing anything to help the Negro masses, but that it has failed to let them know exactly *what* it is doing. It may take a long time for a judicial decision to filter down and be meaningful in the daily existence of the man in the street. And when change does come, he is not always aware of what has been behind the passage and enforcement of this fair employment practices law, or that fair housing statute. The N.A.A.C.P. has not failed the common Negro man, but is has often failed to apprise him of exactly what the organisation is, what it is trying to do, what it has done, and what role it has for him to play. It is hard for most Negroes to identify the glitter and finery of a N.A.A.C.P. yacht party—even if it is a benefit affair—with their situation in the ghetto. The N.A.A.C.P. has been so busy

---

[19] Related by Carl Braden, field secretary of the Southern Conference Educational Fund, Inc., in a speech at Harvard University, February 1962. On the basis of his recent field experience, Mr. Braden also stated that the tendency to turn toward more extreme means of seeking protection and redress is becoming increasingly more widespread among Southern Negroes. Events in April 1963 bore this prognostication out.

fighting for the Negro common man that it has been too busy to tell him about it. The Association is certainly guilty of the charge that it is out of touch with the masses, and in this lies one of its greatest weaknesses. It needs a programme through which more Negroes from all levels of society may be made aware of it and drawn into its activity.

Another source of criticism, though not necessarily a weakness, of the N.A.A.C.P. has been the fact that it has never had a Negro president. The organisation is inter-racial, as well as interfaith. But 90 per cent of the Association's members are Negroes, while a disproportionately high number of the whites in the organisation are in top official posts. The President of the Association is solely a 'titular' head, while the effective leader is the Executive Secretary, an office long held by Negroes. Still, it is often wondered why in its fifty-three years the N.A.A.C.P. has not once seen fit to choose a Negro as its 'titular' head.[20] However spurious, this remains a cause for dissension.

Arthur B. Spingarn, who has been President of the Association for several years, was re-elected to that office in January 1962. It is difficult to explain the N.A.A.C.P. tradition of white presidents; the Association's position is that it is an inter-racial and an integrationist organisation and that considerations of race do not enter into the election of officers. It is true that the average white involved in the organisation is a well-educated, liberal intellectual, and as such is more qualified for high office than the *average* Negro member. This is still no explanation, however. Perhaps in the minds of many the office of president is reserved as an honour for a man who has shown an active interest in the work of the organisation and who has been its benefactor as well. Negro officers in the Association benefit it mainly through their service.

[20] Muslim Minister Malcolm X. for example, states, 'Even if it is just a "titular" position, it seems that it would have gone to a Negro at least once in the last fifty years.' ('The Jerry Williams Show', Radio Station WMEX, 12 January 1962.)

Today the N.A.A.C.P. continues in its traditional course of voicing the American Negro's protest and seeking redress for him from the oppressiveness of a discriminatory system. However, the organisation must be awake to its present weaknesses and to the changing needs and mood of the Negro populace that it purports to represent. It is only in this way that it can expect to remain in the vanguard of the protest movement and hope to maintain its traditional line of success.

The Association was created, in part, as a challenge to the leadership of Booker T. Washington. Washington had achieved the position of being considered *the* spokesman for the Negro. But there were many for whom he did not speak, and they organised to present an alternative to his accommodationist leadership. Some fifty or more years later, the wheel has turned full circle and the N.A.A.C.P. finds itself in a position analogous to Washington's in 1909. The N.A.A.C.P. has long been considered to represent 'the viewpoint of the Negro community' in America. The existence of such a community of opinion is even more of a fiction today than it was in Washington's time. The widest possible spectrum of opinions and positions is found among American Negroes today, and more and more voices of dissent are raised as the N.A.A.C.P. attempts to maintain its role of 'speaking for the Negro'. Many Negroes feel far removed from the problems of Little Rock and Birmingham, and are caught up in their own personal desires for individual fulfilment quite apart from considerations of race. While still more deny that the N.A.A.C.P. speaks for them for other reasons; they see it as too conservative and feel that a more militantly active policy is preferable to the slow legalistic approach which has failed to bring about the desired results. There is a growing disillusionment with the traditional channels of change and a search for new methods that might prove more effective.

Recently, the N.A.A.C.P. has been forced to shift its ground in recognition of the changing times. If it can continue to shift and modify enough, it will not easily be displaced by other groups. Whether it likes it or not, it has been drawn more and more into the direct-action phase of protest. The local branches have been greatly influenced by the advent of wide-scale direct action in the area of Negro protest and in increasing numbers are taking part in and initiating direct-action projects of their own. Local branches of the N.A.A.C.P., in the South especially, have conducted sit-ins, wade-ins and other forms of protest far afield from the traditional N.A.A.C.P. approach. The local N.A.A.C.P. played a large role in the Rainbow Beach wade-ins in Chicago during the summer of 1961. The Association has had to accept these activities of its branches since it would be organisational suicide to do otherwise. It has endorsed the sit-ins and Freedom Rides and accepted the direct-action activities of the branches. However, this put it in an uncharacteristic role of follower rather than leader of Negro protest. Its attempts to identify the current direct-action protest movement with the isolated N.A.A.C.P. Youth Council sit-ins in Oklahoma City during 1958 has been futile. The student non-violent movement is not and will not be considered a N.A.A.C.P. triumph.

The problem of accommodating the new restiveness among American Negro youth is illustrated in its extreme form in the lament of Edward Cooper, executive secretary of the Boston N.A.A.C.P.: 'We have lost some of our best young people from the Youth Council to the Muslims. I just can't understand it.' Unless the N.A.A.C.P. takes note of the fact that a great number of its younger members (and older ones, too) feel that the legalistic approach alone is not doing the job or expressing their protest, the N.A.A.C.P. stands to lose even more ground. Since the new non-violent direct-action protest will never outgrow the need for legal assistance, it is not a question of *either* the N.A.A.C.P. approach *or* the student movement approach, as it was in the case of the polarisation of the Booker T. Washington and N.A.A.C.P. methods; rather is it a question of whether the N.A.A.C.P. can continue to maintain its position of pre-eminence in the area of Negro protest or whether it will have to share its position with another type of protest, quite different from the traditional.

III. WE SHALL OVERCOME

We shall overcome
We shall overcome
We shall overcome—someday
Deep in my heart
I do believe, that
We shall overcome someday.

Old Negro spiritual adopted as a song of the
student protest movement.

ROSA PARKS should have known better. She was no young
woman. She had lived a long time under the laws of the
state of Alabama and the city of Montgomery. She knew
that when the bus driver told her and other Negroes to get
up from their seats and move to the back of the bus to
accommodate white passengers getting on, she should move.
But somehow on 1 December 1955, she could not bring
herself to do it. Rosa Parks would go to jail. She would pay
the fine. And though she did not know it, she would set a
city of 50,000 Negroes walking and trigger off a new form
of Negro protest that would bring into prominence a bright
and dynamic leader—the Reverend Martin Luther King, Jr.

The Montgomery Bus Boycott, 1955–56

Mrs. Parks' arrest was not the cause of the city-wide
bus boycott by Negroes that was to follow, only its pre-
cipitant. The bus service in Montgomery had long been
something that particularly rankled with Negro patrons.
Though they were the major source of the bus line's
customers, they were continually subjected to the indignities
of segregation. There were no Negro bus-drivers, and many
of the white drivers were rude, even abusive:

It was not uncommon to hear them [bus drivers] referring to
Negro passengers as 'niggers', 'black cows', and 'black apes'.
Frequently Negroes paid their fare at the front door, and then were

forced to get off and reboard the bus at the rear. Often the bus pulled off with the Negro's dime in the box before he had had time to reach the rear door.[1]

Word of the arrest of Mrs. Parks aroused the Negro community of Montgomery, who seemed to feel with her, 'We've had enough'. Negro leaders in Montgomery consolidated this opposition and called for a boycott of city buses on 5 December, the day of the Parks' trial. Even the leaders themselves were surprised at the almost 100 per cent effectiveness of the boycott, as nearly empty buses rolled around Montgomery all day. Mrs. Parks was convicted and fined ten dollars, plus court costs. Negroes in Montgomery re-grouped and decided to carry on the protest. The Montgomery Improvement Association was formed, and the Rev. Martin Luther King, Jr. was chosen as its president. King was a young man aged twenty-six, Southern-born, the son of a Baptist minister. He had only recently completed his theological training at Boston University, and had come to Montgomery as pastor of the Dexter Avenue Baptist Church. The faith in the intelligence and dynamism of King which the people displayed was to be justified by the leadership he was to display in the long months ahead.

King believed that it was the responsibility of the people not to lend their co-operation to an 'evil system'. He felt that, 'He who passively accepts evil is as much involved in it as he who helps to perpetrate it. He who accepts evil without protesting against it is really co-operating with it.'[2] The Montgomery Improvement Association mobilised and informed the Negro community. They organised a motor pool to transport those for whom it was impossible to walk back and forth to work, though many did walk—as much as twelve miles daily. One of the sources of greatest surprise to the white community was the speed and effectiveness with which the Negroes organised.

[1] Martin Luther King, Jr., *Stride Toward Freedom*, p.40.
[2] *Ibid.*, p. 51.

The demands of the M.I.A. were simple and direct: (1) a guarantee of courteous treatment; (2) passengers to be seated on a first-come first-served basis, with Negroes seating from the back; and (3) employment of Negro drivers on predominantly Negro bus routes. Week after week Negroes stayed off the buses. There were great mass meetings in which the people came together to sing and pray and to hear suggestions from the leaders. King insisted on a spirited protest, yet one that would leave ground for a proper reconciliation once victory had been achieved. He admonished:

If you will protest courageously, and yet with dignity and Christian love, when the history books are written in future generations, the historians will have to pause and say, 'There lived a great people— a black people—who injected new meaning and dignity into the veins of civilisation'.[3]

King believed in the non-violent direct-action approach of Gandhi and made it a basis for the Montgomery bus strike. He combined the teachings of Gandhi and Christian ethics (more familiar to the Negroes of Montgomery) into a philosophy of direct action for social change:

As I delved deeper into the philosophy of Gandhi my skepticism concerning the power of love gradually diminished, and I came to see for the first time its potency in the area of social reform. Prior to reading Gandhi, I had about concluded that the ethics of Jesus were only effective in individual relationship . . . . But after reading Gandhi, I saw how utterly mistaken I was.

Gandhi was probably the first person in history to lift the love ethic of Jesus above mere interaction between individuals to a powerful and effective social force on a large scale.[4]

King held true to his philosophy throughout the boycott. On numerous occasions, acts of violence on the part of whites caused many Negroes to come to the verge of retaliatory violence, and his power as a leader and his commitment to the philosophy of love and non-violence were most powerfully demonstrated when he quelled an angry and armed

[3] King, *op. cit.*, p. 63.
[4] *Ibid.*, p. 96–7.

mob of Negroes which had formed after the bombing of his home.[5]

Harassment, both official and non-official, were part of the pattern of the opposition over the long months of the boycott. Many persons had their homes bombed. There were the threatening letters and telephone calls. One day King was trailed around the city by policemen, until finally he was stopped and accused of going 'thirty in a twenty-five mile zone'. He was taken to jail, but was released soon afterwards when a cash bond was provided. Later there were mass arrests, King included, for 'conspiracy to prevent the operation of a lawful business, without just cause or legal excuse'. All were found guilty, and the cases were appealed. Later the city started action against the motor pool, as a 'private enterprise operating without a license' and a 'public nuisance'.

All these tactics were to prove of little avail, for on 13 November 1956, almost a year after the boycott had started, the U.S. Supreme Court affirmed the decision of a lower federal court and declared Alabama's state and local laws requiring segregation on buses unconstitutional. The desegregation order was sent to Montgomery. Rosa Parks would not have to move to the rear of the bus.

The success and importance of the Montgomery bus boycott goes far beyond the obtaining of a Supreme Court ruling against segregated transport facilities, important as that was. The Montgomery struggle called forth a great and significant Negro protest leader in the person of Dr. King. It is also important because it captured the attention

---

[5] Quite often the necessity of preventing non-violence from being transformed into violence proved a real test of King's mettle. In this particular case, the ire of the Negroes over the bombing of his home was more than obvious. King reports that when he arrived on the scene, policemen were roughly trying to clear the street, but were being ignored by the crowd. King heard one Negro say to a policeman who was trying to push him aside: 'I ain't gonna move nowhere. That's the trouble now; you white folks is always pushin' us around. Now you got your '38 and I got mine; so let's battle it out.' (King, *op. cit.*, p. 136).

of the nation and the rest of the world and forced people
to take note of some very important flaws in the fabric of
American democracy. Certainly not the least important of
the boycott's effects was the introduction on a wide scale of
a philosophy and form of protest quite new to the American
social scene. Non-violent direct action as a means to social
change caught the imagination and it was through the
dramatic image of King and the passive resistance movement
in Montgomery that the seeds of future protest first became
planted in many people's hearts.

This direct-action protest, though passive, was also
extremely important as an indication of a new and burgeoning militancy on the part of Negroes. Paradoxically, such
passive protest showed white Southerners that the Negro
was no longer as passive as they thought him to be. The
Negro was openly declaring that he would not conform the
patterns of his behaviour to what the whites told him they
should be, but to what he knew was in keeping with the
worth and dignity of the human individual. Montgomery
was an important sign of a great restiveness among American
Negroes and their growing willingness to turn to unfamiliar
and untried ways to express their grievances and to gain
redress.

The Sit-Ins

1 February 1960 is given as the day of the start of the
sit-in movement. While it is true that the current movement
did have its genesis in the sit-in protest of the four North
Carolina agriculture and technical freshmen in Greensboro, North Carolina that day, the sit-in type of protest
is not new to the American scene. There have been individual and group 'sit-ins' in the past. Early seventeenth-
century slave records carry the story of Tony, a Negro slave,
and of his attempts at active non-cooperation as a means of
protest.[6] In 1875, a Negro staged a one-man sit-in at the
Metropolitan Opera House in New York City. The present-

[6] Aptheker, *op. cit.*, pp. 133-134.

day Congress of Racial Equality had its beginnings in a sit-in protest staged in a downtown Chicago restaurant in 1942. In 1958 the Youth Council of the Oklahoma City N.A.A.C.P. started staging sit-ins in their home town. The difference is that the protest of the four students in Greensboro caught on and spread throughout the region spontaneously and extensively, until it appeared that a whole new social movement was taking place. Ezell Blair, leader of the original four in Greensboro, reports that on the day following their initial protest in the Woolworth store there were twenty-one students back at the store. Within a few days the protest had spread to Durham and Winston-Salem. By the end of the month, it had moved to thirty cities in seven states. Two months later, seventy-five cities in twelve states had had sit-ins. Nearly 1,300 arrests had been made by this time; most of these were of Negroes. There were nearly 400 arrests in Orangeburg, about 150 in Nashville, nearly 40 in each of Tallahassee and Florence (South Carolina), about 80 in Atlanta, about 65 in Memphis and nearly 85 in Marshall, Texas. In the North, college students staged supporting demonstrations and raised funds for arrested Southern students. The focus of the sit-ins was broadening to include libraries, museums and art galleries; the methods also were varied, by wade-ins, stand-ins, kneel-ins and other forms of non-violent direct-action protest. The willingness of the students to go to jail for their purpose was another aspect of the protest that was new to the American scene. Going to jail, Thoreau notwithstanding, has always had a serious social stigma attached to it in America. For many of these middle-class American Negro college students this was probably no small hurdle and certainly an even more difficult thing for the parents and elders of these students to rationalise.

The sit-ins spread during 1960. The non-violent direct-action technique was used, and almost without exception when there was violence it was white-instigated and unreturned. During the month of June, U.S. Attorney-General Rogers met with national chain-store managers in order to try to convince them to desegregate facilities in as many cities as possible. This meeting apparently had a great effect on the stores' policies, since many cities began desegregating their lunch counters directly after it. But the stores still did not move to make changes in their Deep South branches. By the end of 1960, just eleven months after the sit-ins began, 126 cities had desegregated facilities in their lunch counters. Many successes had come about through negotiation; there had been demonstrations in only about 100 cities. A year later, in January 1962, the number of 'success cities' was in the neighbourhood of 200. This number is phenomenal, considering the length of time that the sit-ins had been taking place and the firmly-rooted Southern intransigence on this matter—which is considered 'social'.

The final legal question surrounding the sit-ins is still hazy—at least for the moment. On 11 December 1961, the U.S. Supreme Court handed down its first decision in sit-in cases, in which it voided the conviction of sixteen Negro students from Southern University in Baton Rouge, Louisiana who had been convicted of the 'commission of an act in such a manner as unreasonably to disturb or alarm the public'. The court held that the peace had not been disturbed by the students' demonstrations and that their arrest was unlawful. On 25 February 1963 the Supreme Court ruled eight-to-one that 187 Negroes were convicted unjustly on breach of the peace charges filed after they had demonstrated on the South Carolina capitol grounds. Constitutionally protected rights of free speech, free assembly and freedom to petition for redress of their grievances had been abridged, the Court declared. These decisions were seen as tremendous victories for the student movement, especially since these rulings have bearing upon the cases of many other students involved in the protests. The question of conviction under 'trespass' laws and special anti-sit-in laws (passed in some states) remains unclear.

In its earliest days, the sit-in movement was a spontaneous, indigenous student affair, but it was not long before a more strictly organisational approach evolved. The Southern Christian Leadership Conference (S.C.L.C.),[7] under the Rev. Martin Luther King, Jr., formed in 1957, came on the scene to aid this new phase of direct-action non-violence in any way it could. King's group is based in Atlanta, Georgia but has sixty-five groups throughout the South. Most of the important offices in the organisation are held by Southern Negro ministers. S.C.L.C. espouses non-violence as a way of life.

The Congress of Racial Equality (CORE) and the Student Non-Violent Co-ordinating Committee ('Snick') are two other organisations involved which are of at least equal importance with the S.C.L.C. These groups advocate non-violent protest only as a technique, a means to an end, and not necessarily as a way of life. CORE is a national inter-racial organisation, with its main offices in New York City. It has been active in direct-action non-violence since 1942.[8] Throughout the sit-in movement, CORE has played a large and important role in organising, co-ordinating, and advising protest demonstrators.

'Snick' was formed in 1960 and, as its name suggests, took as its original function the co-ordination of the protest work of the many student groups conducting sit-ins. It now initiates protests in Southern communities and is carrying out a voter registration project in Mississippi.[9] It consists of a small hard-core group of militant students or ex-students. The full-time representatives receive sometimes as little as $20 a week for their maintenance while carrying on the field work. 'Snick' has only about forty representatives and is student-controlled. More recently the group has included several adults on its executive board to help advise them;

[7] S.C.L.C., *Southern Christian Leadership Conference*, p. 2.
[8] Congress of Racial Equality, *This Is CORE*, pp. 1–5.
[9] Great emphasis has been placed on voter registration in Mississippi of late. The S.C.L.C. has undertaken a large programme in this field. In addition, two Negro ministers tried to stimulate greater political acitivity by running for Congress in Mississippi in 1961.

included in this group are Ella Baker, formerly with King, and Harry Belafonte, the entertainer.

The many factors at work in American society which have made such a movement possible at this time are not at once easy to define. However, from the vast complex of interacting forces several main lines of influence may be drawn which will help better to explain the existence and the proliferation of the sit-in protest.

The urbanisation and industrialisation of the 'new South' with its concomitant increase in mobility and social fluidity, even within the segregated system, is a leading factor. As the Southern city has grown and prospered it has attracted large numbers of Southerners, white and Negro, to its centre. Over a period of many years there has been a steady increase in urban population in the South as people from the rural and back-country areas have come to the city looking for new opportunities. It has meant for the Negro a higher wage scale, as well as an introduction to a more cosmopolitan atmosphere and the traditional 'American middle-class values'—including the premium placed on education. The children of many of these Negroes are the college students who are actively engaged in the protests of today. As they acquire all the credentials of citizenship and acceptability, they are loath to take the second-rate, second-class citizenship that is proffered to them. In this respect they differ from their fathers before them. The white man's old answers will no longer work in the new generation.

Perhaps the greatest significance of the student non-violent movement lies in the students' rejection of the historical role played by their parents for completely new means of protest. To a great extent, the movement can be seen as a rebellion against parental standards, including their traditional religion. A major portion of these students are the first members of their families to go to college. In college they move in a climate relatively free of parental restraint, and have been able to work out for the first time their own approaches to the problems of discrimination—

approaches that more genuinely reflect their attitudes and their spirit. It is of central importance that we understand both the nature of this rejection and the mood of this present generation of demonstrators—the so-called 'new Negro'.

There is an old Negro spiritual which soulfully repeats the lines 'I'm gonna wait upon the Lord 'til my change comes', and for a long time this has been the attitude of the major portion of adult Negroes in the South. For most, at best, their protest has been conservative support of the traditional legalistic programme of the N.A.A.C.P. At worst, it has been acquiescence in a system that has so beaten them down that they could do little more than submit. The students have come to say that this no longer need be the case. They have taken the initiative, and their protest reflects their belief in Byron's maxim that those 'Who would be free, themselves must strike the blow'—only the 'weapon' they have chosen is non-violence.

In a meeting of student leaders during the height of the sit-in protest in 1960, a Negro youth stood up and voiced this feeling when he said, 'We have been singing and praying for 300 years. Now is the time we should do something ourselves.'[10] Though the protest has had an unmistakeably religious cast from its inception, it is a social gospel with which the students are fired, not the patient religion of Job that claimed their fathers' allegiance.

The mood that prevails among the students is summed up quite well in 'An Appeal for Human Rights', an eloquent manifesto drafted by students of the six Negro colleges in Atlanta, Georgia, and presented to the public through three Atlanta newspapers:

We do not intend to wait placidly for those rights which are already legally and morally ours to be meted out to us one at a time. Today's youth will not sit by submissively, while being denied all of the rights, privileges, and joys of life . . . . [11]

[10] Reported to me by James Laue, present in the meeting.
[11] From 'An Appeal for Human Rights', a paid advertisement in *The Atlanta Constitution, The Atlanta Journal*, and *The Atlanta World*, 9 March 1960.

Conservatism of parents and college presidents was an original obstacle to overcome. State officials put pressure upon administrators of state schools, demanding that the presidents and deans keep the students in line. In many cases, faculty and student leaders at state schools were expelled for participation in the sit-in movement. However, in most cases school officials did not interfere with the protests. The position of Dr. Rufus E. Clement, President of Atlanta University, is typical of many. He affirmed the students' right to protest, and said, '. . . we are not going to tell you what you should or should not do . . .'—this, with the conservative reservation that the students keep their protests within the law, non-violent and free from inter-ference with the academic programme.

Parents often had a difficult time understanding the new way of their offspring—especially on the matter of going to jail. A great deal of opposition grew out of natural parental fear, and not from disagreement with the goals of their children's protest. The decision to follow a 'jail, not bail' policy was often difficult for the student to make. Thomas Gaither, one of the main student leaders, states:

Making a decision to go to jail for the first time was not easy. In some cases, it meant leaving a girl friend; in others, antagonizing parents who had little understanding of non-violent action and much fear for their children's safety . . .[12]

John Gaines, 'jailed-in' with Gaither in Rock Hill, South Carolina, reports:

I don't think I ever got it explained completely to my great-grandmother. She was afraid they'd work me too hard and that I couldn't stand it. She was still puzzled when I told her that it was a privilege for a Negro to go to jail for his rights.[13]

With regard to his grandmother, a cook at the Negro college in Rock Hill, Gaines relates:

She told me I was disobedient when I said I had to go to jail.

[12] Thomas Gaither, *Jailed-In*, p. 5.
[13] John Gaines quoted by Gaither, *op. cit.*, p. 11.

But once I got locked up, she was quite changed. She came to jail and asked me if I was all right or needed anything.[14]

As a further demonstration of family backing when the issue was pressed, Gaines' ninety-five-year old *great*-grandmother came to the prison in her wheelchair on the first visiting day, bringing with her $200 cash, just in case John had changed his mind and would accept bail. Parents, grandparents, and older relatives of student demonstrators all over the South who were at first confused by the new protests readily joined to give the students their backing and encouragement once it was evident what the students were trying to do and how well they were doing it. This combination for solidarity was important not only for student morale and family peace, but was essential for the programmes of economic withdrawal and selective buying central to the students' campaign.

A great desire for equal treatment and a willingness to risk much for it has characterised the student movement throughout. The students have been warned that participation in the sit-ins may be a 'black mark' on the academic records of those who wish to teach or get civil service jobs in the future. Lloyd Williams of South Carolina State College speaks for all those involved in the movement when he answers:

But we are born with a black mark—the color of our skins. We are born second-class citizens, we go to a second-class college, we get a second-class education, and then we go out and teach and give other Negro kids more second-class education. If we don't make a fight for it, we'll never get to be first class.[15]

Likewise, in many ways the sit-in movement can be interpreted as an expression of a typical American middle-class drive for 'acceptance'. It has been pointed out that

[14] Gaither, *op. cit.*, p. 11.
[15] Lloyd Williams, quoted by William Shannon in the *New York Post*, 2 April 1960. Reprinted by The Emergency Public Integration Committee of Boston in a series of *Post* articles by Shannon, 'Sitdown in the South.'

only people who are relatively well off in the first place worry about service and treatment at a lunch counter. To a large extent this is true. Whereas the relative gap between the average white income and the average Negro income has remained about the same over the last decades, the Negro is no longer in a position where mere survival is his paramount concern. His wage today, especially in the industrialised areas, is far above the mere subsistence level—formerly this could not always be said. Now that he is sure that he can get food, the Negro can start to worry about the way in which it will be served to him.

This growing economic strength on the part of the Negro has many other implications which are at once obvious. The buying power of the Negro community represents a crucial factor in the economic system of most Southern areas. The buying power of the Negroes in the United States is about $20 billion (American billion = 1,000 millions), equal to that of the entire nation of Canada. The awakening to the usefulness of this power, first in Montgomery and then in the sit-ins, represents an important step forward in effective protest. By boycott, selective buying and other means, the Negro has found a very useful 'weapon' in his struggle. The campaigns in Nashville, Tennessee and Tuskegee, Alabama are prime examples of the many campaigns of economic withdrawal by Negroes which have been eminently successful. 'Economic withdrawal' rather than 'boycott' is the term preferred by many in the movement. They point out that theirs is a moral crusade and as such should use moral means to achieve its ends. They do not look upon it as punitive action against the offending store-owner, but as a refusal on their part to co-operate with an evil system.

Nashville in 1960 illustrates one of the greatest successes of economic withdrawal. There the withdrawal was maintained at about 98 per cent effectiveness for approximately seven weeks. Nashville is a city in whose stores Negroes spend about $7,000,000 annually. Different stores depend on Negro customers in differing degrees, but for some

receipts from Negro customers represented as much as 40 per cent of total sales. Withdrawal was sure to have an effect on almost all of the city's businesses, however. Negotiations soon started, and a favourable settlement was reached.

While economic factors are under consideration, it should be pointed out that in many ways the students are in a strong position to protest actively since they are both less 'economically vulnerable' and less 'economically responsible'. They do not stand in danger of losing jobs and business patronage as a result of their protest, as would many of their parents; and, in addition, at this stage of their lives most of them do not have the financial responsibilities of family men. They are more mobile and more intimately in tune with the times.

Industrialisation has also made the white community—especially the businessmen—more acutely aware of Northern capital and Northern enterprise. They wish to attract the mills and plant that might be built in their areas and they know that industry avoids racial hot spots. The white community is thus committed to trying to maintain law and order more diligently than has often been the case in the past. In fact, improvement in Southern police protection has been one result of the new forms of protest. Chambers of Commerce and City Councils are more amenable to compromise should any dispute arise. Businessmen are keenly conscious of what happened to business in Little Rock and New Orleans after their disturbances.

It is interesting to note that more than 60 per cent of the sit-in cities have been communities with 50,000 people or more. Only 5 per cent of the protest cities have populations under 10,000.[16] The existence of Negro colleges in the larger communities also accounts for part of this trend.

In addition to urbanisation and industrialisation, the improvement of Negro education is another very important factor. In 1930, only 27,141 Negroes were in college. Today there are more than 200,000—more than the total number

[16] James H. Laue, *Race Relations Revolution: The Sit-In Movement*, p. 31.

of Germans studying in German universities. Improvement in Negro theological training has been another benefit. The growing ranks of the educated Negro has provided a quality of leadership higher than in previous generations; it has also, of course, provided a greater number of qualified leaders.

A third factor is tied up with governmental and legal action. The students were quite young when the 1954 decision was handed down. For most, it was a source of great joy and expectation. The 1954 decision has probably spurred many on in the struggle for *complete* equality before the law; it has also given impetus to many who are impatient with the slow rate of implementation of the desegregation decision.

To some extent, the upsurge of African nationalism has served as a further impetus to the protest of Negroes in America. 1960, the year of the sit-ins, is also known as the African Year, in recognition of the large number of African nations that received their independence then. The feeling is often expressed among American Negroes that, 'If we don't wake up soon, we're going to find that we and the people in South Africa are the only coloured people in the world still not free.' Many American Negroes identify very strongly with the African freedom movement and African students on campuses in the South challenge the American Negro student to act on his own behalf.

Perhaps a little less obvious, but no less real, has been the impact of television on the South. This impact has been twofold. In the first place, it exposes the Southerner to different value alternatives. National television programmes often present social situations that run counter to the accepted way of doing things in the South. The Southerner, white and Negro, sees not only that different approaches to the problem of living together are possible, but that close Negro-white relationships do not always have earth-shattering results. The Yankees and the Red Sox may not be able to play an exhibition baseball game in the city of Birmingham, but nothing the city fathers can do can stop the game from coming into the living room, in black and white, upon the television screen. Southern leaders recognised this 'problem' several years back when the Arthur Godfrey Show had a racially mixed quartet, 'The Mariners', appearing regularly. There were attempts at television blackouts and boycott of the sponsor's product. There have been more recent instances of Southerners taking offence at some television programmes, but the air-wave exclusionist policies seem of little avail. Then, too, television has played a very useful role in spreading the news of protests throughout the South. This has been a means of keeping the Negro in North Carolina aware of what his counterpart is attempting or going through in Louisiana. From such information can come more of a spirit of cohesiveness and 'oneness'.

Not the least among these many factors is the mobility of the present generation of Southerners. Travel and the armed forces have made it possible for many a Negro to 'get around', and quite often after a man has been 'around' a lot he is not willing to accept his old home situation as necessary and static. Southern Negroes travel North to visit relatives who are leaving the South in increasing numbers to settle in Northern cities. In the armed forces they travel around the world and live in integrated situations. This broadening of horizons for the Negro makes it difficult for the old-guard white who wants to 'keep the Negro in his place'. Then, too, as after any war, the men who served in Korea, on their return to the South want a little more of that freedom they fought so hard to protect.

A final source of impetus to the new student protest has been the influence of the Rev. Martin Luther King, Jr. It would be hard to overestimate the power of the image that he has created in most of the students' minds. They all know his story. Following the success of the Montgomery bus strike, the Fellowship of Reconciliation printed and distributed throughout the South, to almost every Negro school, a colourful illustrated booklet on Dr. King and the

Montgomery story.[17] The protest in Montgomery, the
victory in a Supreme Court decision and King himself
captured the imagination of students and adults throughout
the world—but especially of Negro students and adults in
the South. Much of this has worn off now (May 1963), as
many of the more militant students feel that King has not
lived up to his promise as a leader, and is too much involved
in speech-making around the country and not enough
involved in the daily dirty work of testing, protesting and
going to jail. King insists that he has been in jail as much as
anyone and that it is absolutely necessary that he raise
$100,000 a year by speaking.[18] Nevertheless, the fact
remains that King was a very great influence in this
protest. He has shown the students that it can be done, by
proving to them the efficacy of non-violent direct action in
the cause of social reform.

Aside from the gains won in the form of lunch counters
desegregated and favourable court ruling, other less tangible
advances seem to accrue from the sit-in protests. For one
thing, they have had a tremendous educational value. People
all over America and all over the world have become more
aware of the racial situation in America. Many people
who had never thought about what it must mean to be a
Negro there—especially in the South—were awakened for
the first time by the dramatisation of the human element in
the situation before their eyes in sharp relief. The students
caused the question to lose much of its abstractness, and
many people were to think for the first time what it must
mean to a man to move in a world in which he must think
before he sits, wades, kneels or rides. Many people
were made to realise that it was not a syrupy coke or a seat

[17] Laue emphasises the extremely important role played by this 'comic
book' in acquainting Southern Negroes over ten years old with Martin
Luther King and the Montgomery story.
[18] King was arrested for the thirteenth time on 12 April 1963. His
leading role in the demonstrations in Birmingham, Alabama in April–
May 1963 will probably help him recoup some of his earlier loss of
prestige.

at the front of the bus that was at stake, but human dignity.

Significant advances in the realm of interracial communications have also been made as a result of the direct-action non-violent protests. The old 'vertical noise-making'[19] has given way in many communities to a genuine communication between white and Negro leaders on a one-to-one basis around the bargaining table. The white leaders and businessmen must now face the Negroes as men, the mutual creators and shapers of community economic and social policies, and not as mere objects as before.

During the 1960 sit-ins, a police officer was arresting a student sit-in demonstrator in Nashville. He reached in and pulled a slide-rule from the Negro's back pocket. The policeman studied it a moment and then intoned, 'Damn'est knife I ever seen'. However, in spite of how hard the policeman and others like him may try, it is becoming increasingly difficult to hold the old Southern stereotype of the 'violent' but nevertheless 'happy' Negro. Stereotypes have been shattered as legions of American youth have shown the nation a Negro that is neither happy nor violent. Take, for example, this editorial comment from the *Richmond News Leader*:

Many a Virginian must have felt a tinge of wry regret at the state of things as they are, in reading of Saturday's 'sitdowns' by Negro students in Richmond stores. Here were the colored students, in coats, white shirts, ties, and one of them was reading Goethe and one was taking notes from a biology text. And here, on the sidewalk outside, was a gang of white boys come to heckle, a ragtail rabble, slack-jawed, black-jacketed, grinning fit to kill, and some of them, God save the mark, were waving the proud and honored flag of the Southern States in the last war fought by gentlemen. *Eheu!* It gives one pause.[20]

Freedom Rides

Early in the spring of 1961, the Supreme Court in the case of *Boynton* v. *Commonwealth of Virginia* held that discrimination against interstate travellers in bus terminal restaurants is illegal. To test the effects of this ruling CORE

[19] Phrase used by Whitney Young of the Urban League.
[20] From the *Richmond News Leader*, 22 February 1960.

decided to have a 'Freedom Ride', a bus trip through the
South of whites and Negroes who would use the terminal
facilities equally. On 28 April 1961 CORE wrote to the President informing him of their plans.[21] On 4 May a group of
thirteen Freedom Riders, seven Negro, six white, left by
bus for a CORE conference in New Orleans.[22] They
encountered minor difficulties in Virginia all the way down,
but it was not until they reached Alabama that real trouble
broke out. The Riders had separated into two different
buses by now, one a Greyhound, the other a Trailways.
The buses were met at Anniston, Alabama by a mob, which
attacked them. The Greyhound bus was destroyed by an
incendiary bomb and the passengers barely escaped with
their lives. The Trailways bus continued to Birmingham
where the Riders were attacked and beaten upon stepping
off the bus. The U.S. Department of Justice had warned the
Birmingham police that it had received reports of planned
violence when the buses arrived, but no policemen were on
hand at the terminal while the mob had its way.

In the face of the great violence and injury done to its
Riders, CORE called off the rest of their Freedom Ride, and
those who were able continued their journey to New Orleans
by plane. But this was not to be the end of an attempt to
make the Supreme Court ruling meaningful, only the
beginning. The Nashville students non-violent group
took up the Freedom Ride project before the ashes of the
bus at Anniston had grown cold.[23]

[21] Southern Regional Council, *The Freedom Ride*. A special report,
30 May 1961, p.1.
[22] Fifteen years earlier, in 1946, CORE and the Fellowship for Reconciliation staged a Freedom Ride, called then a 'Journey of Reconciliation'
to the upper South to test the Supreme Court decision in the Morgan
case. The decision declared segregation of interstate passengers on buses
illegal, but this first 'Freedom Ride' demonstrated that segregated seating was still enforced and that anyone who challenged segregation was
subject to violence and arrest.
[23] This group of students from Nashville has been extremely active and
effective throughout the protest movement, carrying much more than
its 'share' of the struggle. It is an affiliate of the S.C.L.C. It has in the
person of Diane Nash, formerly of Chicago and Fisk University, one
of the most dedicated and able of student leaders.

A whole new phase of the direct-action non-violent protest was born as people from all over the country, North and South, undertook to Freedom Ride—especially after the Federal Government made it obvious that it would not tolerate violence and disorder made possible through a breakdown in the standard law-enforcing agencies, by sending Federal Marshals into Alabama. After these Marshals were sent into Alabama, Mississippi took all pains necessary to keep law and order in the state. Hundreds of Negro and white Riders coming into Mississippi were arrested quietly and efficiently, almost without incident. That Mississippi justice should function so well was regarded as an achievement in itself.

The Freedom Rides continued throughout the summer of 1961, hoping to 'fill the jails of Mississippi',[24] and eventually to obtain a specific ruling from the Inter-State Commerce Commission in the form of a directive to Southern bus terminals on exactly what they would be required to do under the new desegregation ruling. After a great deal of turmoil, the I.C.C. finally issued a non-discrimination order to bus companies and terminals throughout the land. The order went into effect on 1 November 1961. Another victory had been won. The cases of the hundreds arrested during the Rides are still (May 1963) under litigation and their outcome uncertain, but a Supreme Court ruling on unsegregated transportation service on 26 February 1962 in the case of three Mississippi Negroes makes the Freedom Ride convictions unlikely to stand.

The Freedom Rides are in many ways a direct extension of the other forms of direct-action non-violent protest that had come before. Many of the participants were the same people as the sit-inners. The basic grievance was the same, the ultimate objective in each case similar. One large and

[24] The desire to overtax the resources of the state of Mississippi was to prove unrealistic, since it became obvious that Mississippi had an abundance of jail space, while the Freedom Riders had a paucity of travellers. It was in the end moral and legal pressure that had to be relied upon.

significant difference, however, and one which has caused many people who condoned the sit-ins to condemn the Freedom Rides, is that in the latter a large number of 'outsiders', i.e. not indigenous Southerners were involved. It is argued that the sit-in approach involved members of the community, those who would actually be using the facilities, while many of the Freedom Riders were alien, not only to the community but to the South. Those who support the Rides point out that the very nature of the protest—inter-state travel—called for 'outsiders', and besides, 'how can one be an outsider in one's own country?' it was argued. James Farmer, national director of CORE, said:

Today, how can we think of outsiders keeping hands off injustice in Alabama, when outsiders all over the world can be threatened with destruction by events in a far away place like Laos? How would the dead of Korea view Mississippi's claim that only Mississippians have a right to concern themselves with injustice in that state?[25]

A difference between the sit-ins and Freedom Rides is seen in the fact that in the former hope for success is more largely dependent upon a concentrated effort on the part of the local community, while in the latter the appeal is more to national law and morality, since the demonstrators do not have sufficient numbers or permanence in the community for the long-range economic effect. When worked best, however, the Freedom Rides overcome the natural handicap of being small in number and from without the community by stimulating local protest to act in conjunction with their campaign. This was done in Jackson, Mississippi, for instance, where forty-one Negro citizens of the community joined the Freedom Riders' protest against transportation segregation by sitting-in at the local terminal, and ending up in their home-town jails.

Despite the criticism that has been meted out to them, the Freedom Rides have proved to be the most effective

[25] James Farmer, 'I Will Keep My Soul', *The Progressive*, November 1961.

means of dramatising the situation that existed and of getting enforcement of what the Supreme Court has already declared to be law. Law existing as an abstract right has little worth unless it is made practical and meaningful in a person's real existence. The fact that the law said that U.S. citizens were free to travel without suffering the indignities of segregation did not mean that they were in practice free to travel without discriminatory hindrance. The Freedom Rides went a long way towards making the law a practical reality. The *local* segregation laws which were offensive to travelling citizens from all over the United States were not permitted to stand

As far as working change is concerned, the sit-ins and Freedom Rides have been an immense success. However, all is far from being well. Many a Southern community is still entrenched in its 'way of life'. CORE, S.C.L.C. and 'Snick' are still engaged in the struggle for social justice. For example, in Albany, Georgia local Negroes are still deadlocked with an intransigent City Commission after more than fifteen months of demonstrations and boycotts. The Albany Movement is a city-wide movement of Negroes for the desegregation of public facilities, which has brought hundreds of arrests and has involved most of the leading integration groups, including 'Snick', S.C.L.C. and the N.A.A.C.P. The total involvement of the local community is reminiscent of the Montgomery protest in 1956. In April 1963 the S.C.L.C. under Dr. King's direction began a concentrated drive for desegregation in Birmingham, Alabama—in King's words 'the most thoroughly segregated big city in the U.S. today'—which by now (May 1963) has become the largest demonstration in the history of the civil rights struggle.

Non-violent direct-action projects are still in operation all over the South. There has also been a new emphasis on voter registration and citizenship education drives. Despite continued violence, threats of violence and official harassment, 'Snick' has been bravely carrying out a voter registration project in Greenwood, Mississippi in hopes of raising the number of registered Negro voters there and elsewhere in the state. 'Snick's work in Mississippi has helped to focus the attention of the Federal Government on the voting problem and to bring forth stronger action from the Federal Government for the protection of the prospective Negro voter.

Even where formal concessions have been won complete success has not always followed, for even after a government ruling it is often hard to break old patterns of society and habit learned through oppression. Since the start of the sit-ins in 1960, the movement has met with increasing success and has involved large numbers of both whites and Negroes. It is estimated that over 200 cities have had some kind of non-violent direct-action protest demonstration; there have been 70,000 visible, direct participants; approximately 6,000 different people have been jailed; 140 students expelled; and 60 faculty members fired (mostly at state schools). There have been, of course, numerous cases of personal injury through beatings, high-pressure fire hoses, tear-gas bombs, thrown acid, fire and other methods.

The student movement continues actively today. There is a periodic drop off at exam time and during summer vacation when the students are more dispersed, but this is to be expected: it *is* a student movement.

Of course, there are tensions within the student movement, as well as between it and the larger white community. Many of these take the form of the difficulties often found when protest becomes institutionalised. There are policy disputes, status seekers and organisation men.[26] The

[26] Among students, the number of times they have been in jail is often the key to status. Minor disputes arise from time to time among the students and they exhibit their normal share of human foibles. For many, whose entire life experience has been of 'status deprivation', the new-found importance is something they wish to revel in to the fullest extent.

student movement started off student, spontaneous, unstructured, Negro and indigenous. Organisations, a Northern white liberal press and the adult Negro community have
all become connected in some way with the movement and
brought with them attendant problems. As protest becomes
more of an institution, many students grow impatient with
mailing lists and the exigencies of organisation.[27]

In recent months, 'Snick' has been the most militant of
protest groups, and has striven for a minimum of adult
contact. However, on the whole this dissension in the
non-violence movement has been exaggerated, especially
in the treatment given in the national press to a policy rift
among integrationist groups involved in the Albany protest.
It is unreasonable to think that all Negroes should think
the same—even in matters pertaining to their common
deliverance. Despite tensions, the basic unity of purpose of
the protest groups must not be obscured. In commenting
on the Albany situation Dr. King stated, 'If there was an
indication of division, it grew out of a breakdown in communications. The unity is far greater than our inevitable
points of disagreement.'[28] 'Snick' might feel that the
N.A.A.C.P. is too 'conservative', the N.A.A.C.P. that
'Snick' is too 'headstrong', they both might feel that King
and the S.C.L.C. are trying to take more of their share of
the credit and limelight for the work in Albany, but what-
ever their differences they pale in the face of unity for a
higher goal. Students, adults and all of those actively
concerned in the struggle for equal justice recognise the
paramount importance of co-operation among themselves
and are determined that their voices will not be still as long
as racial inequity exists.

[27] As protest becomes more of an 'exact science' (see C. Eric Lincoln,
'Strategy of a Sit-In') many students feel that it will lose its vitality
along with its spontaneity. 'Snick' is particularly wary of this danger.
The current question asked by active student protesters of the hangers-on
and those who profess to be with the movement 'in spirit' is, 'Where is
your body?'—a challenge to action in the field.
[28] *New York Times*, 19 December 1961.

IV. LET MY PEOPLE GO[1]

What happens to a dream deferred?
Does it dry up
Like a raisin in the sun?
Or fester like a sore—
And then run?
Does it stink like rotten meat
Or crust and sugar over—
Like a syrupy sweet?
Maybe it just sags
Like a heavy load.
Or does it explode?

LANGSTON HUGHES

Behold, I will send you Elijah the prophet before
the coming of the great and dreadful day of the
Lord.   Malachi iv. 5

BOTH the National Association for the Advancement of
Colored People and the non-violent direct-action groups
are motivated by a desire to see the American promise
fulfilled. Their ultimate goal as organisations is to go out of
existence, for they are working for the day when groups
of their nature will no longer be necessary and men be able
to move in society without the hindrances of racial prejudice
and discrimination.

Not all Negroes, however, share the integrationist motives
of these groups. For many it is no longer possible to believe
in the so-called American dream or the white man's good
intentions for an honest democracy. The force of oppression
has turned such people in on themselves and their voices of
protest have quite another sound, their solutions quite
another tenor. Black nationalist organisations claim the
membership of thousands of Negroes in the U.S.A. and

[1] This chapter is the result of extensive research on and among the
Black Muslims, supplemented by two books, C. Eric Lincoln's *The
Black Muslims in America* and E. U. Essien-Udom's *Black Nationalism*,
which appeared while this work was in progress.

the number whose lives and thought are in some way directly influenced by these groups is probably in the millions.

Many, though not all, of these groups are separationist in policy, while others lay emphasis on a type of cultural chauvinism.[2] By far the largest and most influential of these militant black nationalist organisations is The Lost-Found Nation of Islam in the Wilderness of North America— known commonly as the Black Muslims. Since the middle of the 1950s, when their meteoric upsurge in membership began, the Muslims have exercised an increasingly important influence upon the nation's racial scene. The movement is significant both in what the mere existence of such a group indicates about American society and for the insights it gives into the mood of a large segment of the American Negro community.

Though it is only in recent years that the Black Muslims have attained their greatest strength and influence in the area of Negro protest, the search for their beginnings takes us back several decades. The history of the modern Black Muslim movement begins some time in the summer of 1930 when a mysterious pedlar appeared on the streets of Detroit. He seemed to be of Arab origin, but to this day no one has proved his racial or national background. He sold goods in the Negro section of the city and was patronised by the women, who were interested in his exotic wares:

He came first to our houses selling raincoats, and then afterwards, silks. In this way he could get into the people's houses, for every woman was eager to see the nice things the peddler had for sale. He told us that the silks he carried were the same kind that our people used to wear in their home country, and that he was from there. So we asked him to tell us about our own country.[3]

So great was the interest in the preaching of this man that a hall had to be rented for special meetings. He taught

[2] In New York City the Cultural Association for Women of African Heritage and the Order of Danbhala Ouedo are examples.
[3] Quoted in E. D. Beynon, 'The Voodoo Cult Among Negro Migrants in Detroit'.

first from the Bible and then gradually groped his way towards a highly personal interpretation of the Holy Scriptures, and finally to an outright attack on biblical teaching. Slowly he evolved a doctrine of his own (though biblical authority is to this day still given some weight if properly interpreted by the Ministers). The hall in which the meetings were held was named 'Temple of Islam' (now Temple 1) and there the Black Muslim movement in America was born.

In 1934 this esoteric Detroit cult had collected 8,000 members, when in June of that year Mr. Farrad Mohammad, the mysterious pedlar who had initiated the movement, disappeared. Exactly what happened to him is not known. After Farrad Mohammad's disappearance, the direction of the movement fell to his first lieutenant, Elijah Muhammad (Elijah Poole), then a young man in his thirties. In less than three decades after taking control, Elijah has directed and transformed the movement from an esoteric Negro cult in the slums of Detroit to a nation-wide sect with mass appeal, one which claims over a quarter-million members (in fact it has probably no more than 100,000 at most) in twenty-seven states and is recognised by many as a sect of orthodox Islam.

The building process was a slow one for Elijah. In the early days there was trouble with the police and local school officials over his operation of parochial schools for Muslim children. Various interest groups, including the Communists and union-busting elements, tried to use this convenient enclave of Negroes to their advantage. The movement has, however, successfully resisted these pressures and at all times has refused to veer from its sole purpose of uplifting the black man in America.

From 1942 to 1946 Elijah was in a federal prison for seditious statements he allegedly made, identifying the Negro's best interest with a Japanese victory in the Second World War. There was no major significant breakthrough in the growth of the movement until the mid-fifties, when Elijah got a column, 'Mr. Muhammad Speaks', in the

Pittsburgh Courier and other Negro newspapers. This was the first time that he had been presented to the Negro public through mass communications media. There was an immediate upsurge in the enrolment of the movement. When the Negro press finally decided to drop Mr. Muhammad's column, his success was already assured; and shortly after the great upswing in membership the national press began to give the movement coverage. There seems to be little doubt that the coverage the movement has received from press, radio and television has served to attract more people into its ranks. Those making up the bulk of its membership are the young, the disillusioned recent immigrant from the South, the low-income urban worker and the socially-rejected in general—those with least to lose from the stigma of being Black Muslims. The frequent observation that this movement has its primary appeal among the low socio-economic class of urban Negroes tells us little, since the vast majority of American Negroes belong to this socio-economic class anyway and are now largely city dwellers.

Beliefs and Goals

Muslim doctrine starts with the premise that the black man in America can never expect equal treatment, since the white man has no intention of ever giving it to him. This hits a responsive note in the hearts of many Negroes, whose experience reinforces this assumption. In denying America's good 'intentions' toward the Negro, Malcolm X., leader of the New York temple, says:

Do you mean to tell me that in a powerful country like this, a so-called *Christian* country, that a handful of men from the South can prevent the North, the West, the Central States and the East from giving Negroes the rights the Constitution says they already have? No! I don't believe that and neither do you. No white man really wants the Black Man to have his rights, or he'd have them. The United States does everything else it wants to do.[4]

4 Quoted in Lincoln, *op. cit.*, p. 19.

The Black Muslims' solution to the American Negroes' problems is separation; they insist on the term 'separation' rather than 'segregation' in order to avoid the racist charges that are made against them. 'Separation', they hold, is something that is done to equals, with no implication of 'superior' or 'inferior', as is the case with segregation. They see American society as sick and point to the damaging effects of the slave mentality which they feel still prevails in the Negro community. They often refer, metaphorically, to Elijah as the physician who can cure the Negroes' socio-economic ills. But in order to do this he must first separate the Negro from the malignant influences of the dominant white society. The white man has made separation a fact, the Muslims now call for *total* separation, as a virtue. While the integrationist groups which we have discussed seek to correct some of the flaws in American life, the Muslims embrace a much nore ambitious goal—they hope to reconstitute a whole society. To do this they feel that they must reconstruct the whole man. The American Negro must be completely made over. He must become a Muslim—a Black Muslim—and a follower of the Honourable Elijah Muhammad.

Elijah has set forth a twelve-point programme for the deliverance of the American Negro. His awareness of the economic precariousness of the American Negro masses is reflected in several points. The programme commands:

(1) Separate yourself from your slavemaster.
(2) Pool your resources, education and qualifications for independence.
(3) Stop forcing yourselves into places where you are not wanted.
(4) Make your own neighbourhood a decent place to live.
(5) Rid yourselves of the lust for wine and drink and learn to love self and kind before loving others.
(6) Unite to create a future for yourself.
(7) Build your own homes, schools, hospitals and factories.
(8) Do not seek to mix your blood through racial integration.

(9) Stop buying expensive cars, fine clothes and shoes before being able to live in a fine house.
(10) Spend your money among yourselves.
(11) Build an economic system among yourselves.
(12) Protect your women.

Disillusionment with America has also caused the Muslims to reject America and their citizenship. Malcolm X. repeatedly makes the claim that 'there are no degrees of citizenship. Either you are a citizen or you are not. There is no such thing as a second-class citizen'. The alienation which members of the movement seem to feel is reflected by the answer Malcolm gave when he was asked whether the fact that he was born in America did not make him an American citizen. He replied, 'Just because a cat has kittens in an oven, it doesn't make them biscuits.'[5]

In order to fulfil their desires, the Muslims say that they must have land of their own. They wish to separate and form a black nation within the United States. The Muslims repeatedly make the cry 'Give us some land!' and say that the United States owes them this concession as back-wages for the 200-plus years that America benefited from the Negro's involuntary free labour. In a debate at Harvard University Malcolm X. outlined some of the details of the Muslim request. He said that the Muslims wanted some land, some tools and a Federal Government subsidy for twenty to twenty-five years, in order to get the nation established. Mr. Muhammad explains the importance of land to the Muslims by saying:

We must become as a people, producers and not remain consumers and employees. We must be able to extract raw materials from the earth, manufacture them into something useful for ourselves. This would create jobs in production. We must remember that without land there is no production.[6]

[5] Minister Malcolm X., Boston University Human Relations Center, speech, 15 February 1960.
[6] 'Mr. Muhammad Speaks', *Los-Angeles Herald-Dispatch*, 26 November 1960. Also in *In Your Midst—Mr. Elijah Muhammad*, booklet published by Temple 11, Boston. Muhammad says: 'The *Black Man* in America

In this rejection of white American society the Muslims include a rejection of their 'Christian-slavemaster' last names. Their former last names are replaced by the letter 'X', which to them represents the fact that, because of the white man, they do not know their true last names but only those that have come down to them from slavery. As the number of people with the same first name in each individual temple increases, a numerical prefix is added to the letter 'X' to distinguish one John or James from another—thus, John 3X. or James 6X. For identification purposes in the society at large, a Muslim will often sign his former last name, preceded by the 'X'—thus Louis X. Smith. Here the Muslim will tell you that the 'X' means 'no longer' or 'ex'.

Not only does the Muslim reject white American society, but he rejects the white man as well. To the Black Muslim the white man is anathema. In his religious mythology the white man is equated with the devil or the forces of evil. The Muslim examines the condition in which he finds himself and his fellow Negroes in America and reasons that someone is to blame for the situation. Once he has gone that far, it is a short step to say that 'it is the white man's fault that we are in the condition that we are'—and to hate him for it. The Muslims make no attempt to follow Dr. King's command to hate the evil without hating the evil doer. The Muslims revel in racial glorification of the black man.

A third area of rejection is Christianity. It is cast off as a 'white man's religion', a tool of colonialism and the stifler of the proper manly and militant virtues. The Muslims make constant references to the deceitfulness of the Christian missionaries in Africa. They repudiate the doctrine of a heaven or after-life and say that it has been used as an

has been too long treated as a pariah, despised, neglected, and left to despair, in a country whose soil his blood, tears, and sweat have nurtured. He must therefore begin building enterprises as his own as the first step toward the eventual unity of Black Men.'

instrument of subjection of the African, as well as the
American Negro. While the Negro's eyes were planted on
the heavens and his soul wrapped up in the expectation of
some far-distant joy at the end of his life, the white man was
busy scraping up the Negro's gold and looking after his
own more immediate desires of earthly pleasure. The Muslims show a great deal of contempt for the 'turn the other
cheek' doctrine of many integrationists. They are trained
never to initiate a struggle, but to be prepared to defend to
the death (literally) their principles and their women.

The religion of Islam is meant to replace Christianity.
The followers become Muslims and must submit themselves
to the will of Allah. They are expected to follow the teachings of the Holy Koran and to observe the proper dietary,
fasting, bathing and praying obligations. Elijah Muhammad
made a pilgrimage to Mecca in 1960 and was received by
some of the leading Imams of the Islamic religion in the
Middle East. There are several points, however, at which
the Black Muslims deviate from orthodox Muslim teaching.
The most serious of these are their racist doctrines and their
deification of Mr. Farrad Mohammad, founder of the
movement. Farrad is believed to have been the incarnation
of Allah, who made an appearance upon the earth in order
to give Elijah the 'truth' necessary for the salvation of the
black man in the 'wilderness of North America'. This is
one reason that Elijah is regarded so highly by his followers.
He is 'the Messenger' who has received the message directly
from God.

Organisation

Elijah Muhammad is a frail little man in his sixties. He
is a native son of Georgia, the son and the grandson of
Baptist ministers. From his Chicago residence he superin-
tends one of the fastest growing movements in America.
Elijah has the absolute and final word on everything pertaining to the actions of the Black Muslims in America.
However, the ministers of the individual mosques are highly

enough trained and there are enough 'organisation men'
under him for Elijah simply to sit back and play the father-
role to thousands of black men.[7]

Exactly how many thousands is extremely difficult to
judge. Minister Malcolm X. says, 'Those who say, don't
know; those who know, don't say'. And this is quite true.
Because of the secretiveness of the Muslims about such
matters, all figures relating to them have to be speculative.
Dr. Lincoln puts the figure at 100,000. Dr. Essien-Udom,
who has had a great deal of personal contact with the
Muslims, has said that although their rate of conversion is
very high, so is the rate of turn-over—i.e. many 'converts'
do not stay practising Muslims for very long. This may be
because the discipline is too rigid, because of the social
stigma attached to being a Black Muslim, or for some other
reason. At any rate, Dr. Essien-Udom estimates (1962) that
there are only about 15,000 registered, *fully active* Muslims,
about 50,000 professed believers, and a much greater number of sympathisers. Although this estimate of fully active
members might be slightly low, Dr. Essien-Udom's figures
probably come closer to a realistic picture. The Chicago,
New York and Boston Muslim followings are supposed to
be among the largest in the country, but a visitor cannot
help being struck by the very low seating capacity in what
are supposedly three of the movement's leading mosques.
The *total* seating capacity for all three probably does not
exceed 2,500, which give added weight to Dr. Essien-Udom's
belief that it is a small hard core of believers who are the
life of the movement and who have attracted most of the
attention. Not that the attention paid to the Muslims is
unjustified because of their lack of great numerical strength:

[7] There is ample evidence to show that an additional reason for the Hon.
Elijah Muhammad's not being seen in public more often is that his
health is failing. More than once in recent years he has failed to put in
an appearance at important Muslim conferences where he had been
scheduled to address his followers. The question of the line of succession
remains unclear; Elijah's position is unique since he alone has had 'direct
divine revelation'. It is not known whether the leadership will stay in
Elijah's family or go to his chief minister, Malcolm X.

for every person who has made and kept the commitment to the Nation of Islam there are many more who sympathise with his views.

Each of the eighty temples or mosques is, to a great degree, an autonomous unit. It has its own sub-groups, usually consisting of 'The Fruit of Islam' and the 'Muslim Girls Training and General Civilisation Class'. The Fruit is a para-militaristic group of young Muslim men who train and drill for physical fitness and act as guards in the temple. This élite corps of Muslim males helps to keep internal discipline and is ready if outside protection is needed. They act as body-guards for visiting Muslim dignitaries and inspect the proposed itinerary of Mr. Muhammad before any visit, in much the same way as the U.S. Secret Service men act for the President of the United States. The amount known about the inner workings of this group is limited since it is a secret (the Muslims say 'private') organisation which refuses to discuss its activities or to permit outsiders at its meetings.

The Muslim Girls Training and General Civilisation Class is open to the women of the temple. It emphasises the arts of home-making and attempts to teach the young Muslim girl to be a good Muslim mother. Women are held in very high regard by the Muslims. They stress the key role that women play in the training and upbringing of men. Elijah often says, 'A nation can rise no higher than its women'.

In the areas where there are Muslim temples there will always be found Muslim-run businesses and it is Muslim policy to urge members to 'buy black' and 'hire black'. There are Muslim restaurants, barber shops, grocery stores, cleaners and other types of business establishments. In Chicago there is even a Muslim department store. The Muslims own farms both in the Mid-West and in the South. In Georgia they have trucks which deliver fresh fish daily from the sea to their inland markets.

The Muslims have their own parochial schools, some of which are state accredited—as in Detroit and Chicago where Muslim children attend the temple school rather than the public schools of the city. In areas where the schools are not accredited, Muslim children attend the schools of the temple in their spare time and on Saturdays. In the accredited Muslim schools the children attend classes fifty weeks of the year, and start to learn Arabic ('the language of their fathers') in the third grade. Race history is emphasised along with the more standard course of study.

The 'history' that is taught in the Black Muslim movement is often no more than a glorified racial mythology. Muslims reject the term 'Negro' as a description of themselves and other American coloured people, saying that the word is the invention of the white man used to make subjugation of coloured peoples easier. They connect the introduction and usage of the term 'Negro' with the coming of slavery to America. They say this appellation tells nothing of the history and rich cultural heritage of the black race, for it is nothing more than an indiscriminate lumping together of peoples, disconnecting them from any cultural heritage, obscuring past grandeur.

Muslims believe literally that the 'so-called American Negroes' are descendants of 'original man' (the white race is a later mutation), and that they are part of the ancient lost tribe of Shabazz which made its home along the banks of the Nile and in the region of what was later to be Mecca. There is a great attempt at identification with the Nile civilisations that flourished in the past.

Race history as taught by the Muslims is distorted. However, there is some basis in fact for many of their claims, facts that are wide open to Muslim over-amplification. There is evidence of the past existence of relatively advanced 'Negro' civilisations on the lower Nile. During the Middle Ages, there were also large empires of Islamised Africans in the western Sudan. The University of Timbuktu was an important centre of Muslim learning. The pilgrimage to

Mecca of the African leader Mansa Musa of the empire of Mali in the fourteenth century is still famous in the annals of African history. Mansa Musa caused quite a stir during his visit to the East. He flooded the Egyptian market with so much gold that there was a mild inflation after his arrival.

The belief that Negro origins lie in the East is also reflected in the oral tradition of many West African groups today who hold that their ancestors came to West Africa in ancient times as part of a great migration from the East. It is likewise true that there were African Muslims among the slaves brought to this country, but the number would have to have been very small, since Islam had not made inroads into the areas from which most of the slaves bound for America were taken.

The Muslims have learned well the lesson of mass communications media. They are now applying it with the greatest of zeal in the hope of expanding their membership. Mr. Muhammad has a weekly radio programme on many of the radio stations in the different metropolitan areas of the country. His column, 'Mr. Muhammad Speaks' is still carried in some Negro newspapers, and the movement now publishes several newspapers and magazines of its own.

Also listed in the catalogue of organs of propaganda is the theatrical production, *Orgena* ('A Negro' spelled backwards). This show was written, directed, and starred in by Louis X., minister of the Boston temple. Louis, upon being converted to Islam (he was previously Episcopalian), left a $500-a-week career as a popular calypso singer to take $70 a week as a Muslim minister. He vowed at this time never to perform again except in the cause of Islam. His own creation now gives him that opportunity. The show consists of a musical dramatisation of the history of the Negro, 'from the banks of the Nile to the ghettos of America', and a one-act play called *The Trial*, in which the person on trial is the White Man. The verdict is 'guilty' and the sentence is 'death'. The three-hour show is supposed to be both 'entertaining and enlightening'. It has been presented at Carnegie Hall in New York, Symphony Hall in Boston, and in other major cities in the East and Mid-West.

The Muslims have recognised, explicitly or implicitly, the economic precariousness and psychological deprivation faced by the masses of Negroes in American urban areas. They have attempted to provide remedies both for the body and the spirit of the black man. In exchange for economic insecurity, they have offered him the opportunity to join them in their attempts at economic independence. They have set up and run hundreds of business establishments—hiring Muslim and non-Muslim alike. They have opened job opportunities for many—and not in the self-seeking spirit of exploitation but with a feeling for unity, strength, co-operation and mutual assistance.

They have provided thousands of men and women with a sense of identity and moral direction where in many cases there had been ·only the empty blackness of the ghetto. Without doubt, and almost without exception, when a person becomes a Black Muslim there is a great perceptible change. The emphasis on morality and strict discipline creates a new kind of demeanour. The Black Muslim as found in the 'Negro' areas of large American cities is usually more courteous, neater and more respectful of himself and his neighbours than most of those around him.

The existence of this well-disciplined self does not negate the Muslim's militancy, but illustrates that it is not expressed in any overt boisterous manner. The Muslim appears to be in complete control of himself. He moves with a quiet determination and an inner sense of personal dignity. Perhaps, to a large degree, this stems from the race pride that has been instilled in him by the teachings of the movement and its emphasis upon a knowledge of self. Juvenile delinquency among Muslims is negligible, and the members of the family unit seem to find it easier to assume the traditional roles with father as breadwinner and mother as homemaker.

Muslims have succeeded in changing the ways of living of many convicts and ex-convicts. Muslims proselytise inside as well as outside prison walls (see below, p. 77). They have taken into their ranks the prostitute, the dope addict and other deviant or 'marginal' types and transformed them. Muslim leaders often say that the Government owes them a debt of gratitude for the job they have done in the social rehabilitation of 'hopeless' cases and for the money that they have saved public institutions in doing so. Indeed, it is true that one of the facts that is most striking to observers is the great effect that becoming a Muslim has on the lives of individuals.[8] The Muslims open their arms to the rejects of society, because they themselves have rejected society.

For those who follow him, Elijah Muhammad has succeeded in his grand design of drawing Negroes out from the dominant white society and providing a meaningful existence as free as possible from white contact. But he is not satisfied with this partial success. He claims that land is available to him outside America (presumably somewhere in the Middle East) if he desired to set up his black nation today. He refuses to do this, saying that his goal is not some quarter-million 'saved' American Negroes, but every last American black man who suffers under the 'pharaohs' in the 'wilderness of North America'. Elijah Muhammad and the other leaders of the movement tell the American Negro that the solution to the nation's racial problem lies not in efforts to 'integrate' American society, but in *separation* from the white man, and in black unity.

[8] George S. Schuyler, New York editor of the *Pittsburgh Courier*, and one of the most widely read Negro journalists, wrote in his column: 'Mr. Muhammad may be a rogue and a charlatan, but when anybody can get tens of thousands of Negroes to practice economic solidarity, stop crime, juvenile delinquency and adultery, he is doing more for the Negro's welfare than any current Negro leader I know.' *Pittsburgh Courier*, 12 September 1959. One is hard pressed to find evidence to show that Mr. Muhammad is either rogue or charlatan. For an estimation of the man's personal qualities quite different from Mr. Schuyler's, see James Baldwin, 'Letter from a Region in My Mind', *New Yorker*, 17 November 1962.

Muslims and the Public

Because all temple meetings are closed to whites, the impression that most of the general public have received of the Muslims comes from the mass public meetings that the Muslims hold from time to time. The press, radio and television coverage of these mass rallies has consistently presented a distorted image of the Muslim movement and has tended to seize on the more bizarre and fantastic elements and to overplay them.[9] The vehemence of the attack upon whites coming from the lips of these Negroes is shocking even to the veteran ears of seasoned white reporters. Mr. Muhammad's theme of 'separation or death', which is constantly reiterated at mass rallies, has caused a great deal of misunderstanding. While most have interpreted this as a Muslim threat and reported that the Muslims seek the 'extinction of the white race', Elijah Muhammad has insisted that this is a religious doctrine and simply means that God (Allah) will destroy the wicked slavemasters of America unless they 'let my people go', in much the same way as He has destroyed wicked rulers in the past. Similarly, the final 'Battle of Armageddon' must be understood in a religious context as a war in which the forces of good will destroy the forces of evil. It has been wisely remarked that Elijah very carefully treads the line between religious licence and political sedition.[10]

[9] A good deal of attention has been paid in the press to the appearance of George Lincoln Rockwell, leader of the American Nazi Party, at a large Muslim rally. See especially 'The Black Crusade', *Sunday Times Colour Magazine*, 21 April 1963. While it is true that the Nazis and Muslims have openly expressed sympathy for each other's views on racial separation, this has never amounted to total endorsement. Unwarranted importance has been attached to the fact that Rockwell spoke at this rally—this was an open meeting, and the Muslims offered the platform to *all* solutions of America's racial problems. Rockwell simply availed himself of the opportunity—he is grateful for any platform he can get.

[10] Minister Malcolm X. admitted to me that since the forces of evil are represented by the white man and Christianity, and the forces of good by the black man and Islam, the Black Muslim doctrine of the Battle of Armageddon actually amounts to a prediction of an ultimate race

Most of the Black Muslim energy is directed toward a day-to-day effort on behalf of the unity and uplift of the Negro in America, but on several occasions in recent years events have catapulted the Muslims into the national spotlight. During Fidel Castro's visit to New York City in 1960 Malcolm X. was reported to have had a prolonged and closed consultation with the Cuban leader at a time when no one else was being permitted to see him. Reports intimated that there might have been some sort of alliance or negotiations between the two men. The truth of the matter, according to Malcolm, was that he was a part of the host committee in Harlem, and it was for this reason that he was allowed into the Hotel Theresa in Harlem to speak with Castro. He says that his visit was a brief one and not a prolonged 'session'. The Muslims are suing the Hearst newspaper syndicate for $3 million for the erroneous and misleading accounts of this event.

Early in 1961 when a group of American Negroes demonstrated at the United Nations in protest at the murder of Congolese leader Patrice Lumumba and continued colonial activity in Africa, the Black Muslims were blamed. The New York Police Commissioner attributed the disturbance to the Muslims and it was so reported in the papers and by U.N. Ambassador Stevenson. The Muslims contend that they were not involved in the incident and maintain that other black nationalist groups were responsible. This insistence seems more plausible in the light of past Muslim policy on non-intervention in political matters. At any rate, another lawsuit by the Muslims has been instigated as a result of these allegedly slanderous statements.

On occasion, the Muslims have run into difficulty in exercising their right to practise their religion. In New

war in which the white man will be extinguished. When questioned on white Muslims, Malcolm insisted that he has never known any. 'A Muslim is one who submits himself to the will of Allah', he said, 'and I have never known a white man that would truly submit himself to Allah'. Muslims in the Middle East are not white men, he claims. The Black Muslims classify all non-whites as 'black men'.

York state, Muslim prisoners in some of the state penal institutions have been denied the right to practise their own particular brand of Islam. The Muslims have appealed to a higher court. In March 1961 Monroe, Louisiana, one of the thirty cities in Southern and border states with Muslim temples, was the scene of a police raid on a Muslim meeting. Several Muslims were beaten and jailed. They were charged with disturbing the peace, aggravated assault and aggravated battery. This case also has been appealed.

On 27 April 1962 the Black Muslims again came suddenly to public notice in an internationally-reported incident. The incident started when two white Los Angeles policemen decided to question two Negro men who were selling clothes from a parked car on a Los Angeles street. The exact sequence of events that followed is still a matter of dispute, but an altercation developed and a group of Muslims intervened on behalf of the two Negro men stopped for questioning. In the ensuing fray seven Muslim men were shot (one of them killed) and thirteen others arrested and charged with 'resisting arrest' and 'assault'. The two policemen, along with dozens of re-enforcements, entered a nearby Muslim mosque, disrupting a service in progress, and searched for a gun that they had heard was hidden there. No weapon of any kind was found. As the trial of the arrested Muslims approaches (May 1963) there is a great deal of public interest in the case—not least because of the shooting of the seven Muslims, all of whom were unarmed in accordance with their Black Muslim teaching (which does not permit members to carry weapons of any sort).

Despite the Muslims' claim that they eschew all weapons, the Los Angeles police have also alleged that the minister of the Los Angeles mosque is guilty of shooting a police officer during the dispute. However, the arrest of the mosque minister on an 'assault with intent to commit murder' charge was not made until several months after the incident had taken place and the other thirteen Muslims arrested.

Recent years have also seen the upsurge of African nationalism exert an increasing influence upon the Black Muslims in America. They identify very strongly with the rising African nations and their militant leaders—especially when that leader happens to be Muslim, like Sékou Touré of Guinea. When African leaders come to the United States they sometimes meet Muslim leaders. Such has been the case with President Nkrumah of Ghana and Jaja Wachuku, then Speaker of the Nigerian House of Representatives.

On the domestic political scene the Muslims took a sudden new approach after their annual convention early in 1963. In the past, they had avoided American politics as just another part of the corrupt, decadent unjust American system. In their new line, however, the Muslims show themselves a great deal less alienated and less politically unconcerned than before. By their new acceptance of the political process they demonstrate further that theirs is not in fact a total, out-of-hand rejection of the larger society, but merely a response to the injustice they find in that society. The shift in approach probably reflects a greater awareness of the role politics has to play in social change, or at least it reflects a Muslim awareness of their growing power to influence patterns of thought in the Negro community. The Muslims have begun calling to American Negroes to close their ranks and in the coming 1964 elections to elect candidates 'of their own choosing instead of merely existing under those chosen for them by the whites'. Malcolm X. has declared:

Twenty million Negroes can tip the political scales in any direction they choose to leap. That's why Mr. Muhammad says we must select candidates from those who honestly represent the black man, and can be trusted to look after his interests. Yes, even from among Christians.[11]

Implicitly, this is saying, 'Yes, even from among the white man'—a new departure altogether for the Muslims; in the

[11] *Sunday Telegraph*, 24 March 1963.

past, one of the Muslim reasons for ignoring American
politics was their belief that no white man could be trusted.
Malcolm has also said that the Muslims can already
'handle' the Negro U.S. Congressman Adam Clayton Powell
and 'a number of other Negro politicians'. This, of course,
depends upon what Minister Malcolm means by 'handle',
but it is quite true that Powell must take the Muslims into
account because of the great power and influence they wield
in his Harlem constituency.

The Muslim programme as presented to its Negro
audience calls for land so that they may set up a black
nation within the United States. There is much to indicate,
however, that this is a public statement of a goal that Muslim
leaders do not expect to obtain, at least not in the near
future. There are, of course, different levels of communication. What the Muslim leaders tell their Negro following,
what they tell the general public and what they say among
themselves may often be quite different. It seems difficult to
believe that Elijah Muhammad, Malcolm X., and other
Muslim leaders actually believe that the Federal Government is going to give them three, four, five, or *any* number
of states (see above p. 74). Much of present Muslim activity
contradicts a real belief in this goal. All over the country
Muslims are investing and building up their interests. In
Baltimore a large recreation centre 'to keep black children off
the streets' is being constructed; in Chicago plans are
complete for a $20 million Islamic centre, complete with
school, hospital and mosque. All this activity does not seem
the work of a group that expects to be moving out into one
geographical area. A man expecting to move into a new
house does not expend large amounts of money, time and
energy lavishly furnishing the old. But nor does he neglect
the paintwork of the present house, Malcolm is quick to
point out. However, it would seem, that the Muslims
have found this concept and goal of 'nation' a very useful
one, because it has a romantic and unifying power—and

unity and advance seem to be the Muslims' real primary goal, not nationhood.

What the Muslims are developing are communities within larger communities. The way in which they qualify their doctrine of *apartheid* is very interesting. The Muslims ask for separation, but the request is for land in the United States. They do not have the 'back to Africa' intentions of the Garvey movement of an earlier day. While they supposedly reject the white man and his ways, the Muslims will often use the white man's values as their criteria. Thus, there is the emphasis on running one's business well, 'like the white men do'. Muslim standards of dress and behaviour as symbols of 'having arrived' come straight out of Madison Avenue and a Puritan morality. Of course, for Muslims 'arrival' means a different thing than for most people. It means the coming of their knowledge of the true nature of their condition and of the way out of it through the teachings of the Honourable Elijah Muhammad. The Muslims purport to be separationists, but time and time again they will lament the failing of integration and point to it as the reason for their position. Theoretically, as separationists, they should be pleased when integration does not work.[12]

Nevertheless, the facts must be faced: the Muslims are a group with views which can be described in no other way than 'extreme racist', and those who condemn racism in other forms must find the Muslim doctrines unpalatable. It is also true that much of what spurs on the Muslims is a fierce hate for the white man—'the devil'. But there is a difference. If there is hate, it is 'the hate that hate produced' —hate, or indifference, which may be worse. A nation that too long rejects its own can expect one day to find

[12] In the teachings at temple meetings and in my talks with Muslim ministers and followers, I have often found this contradiction between attacking the idea of integration and at the same time lamenting its failure to work. Malcolm X. and others have admitted to me that what they really want is complete equality—*now*. But since the Government has not seen fit to guarantee this equality immediately the Muslim can no longer wait, and embraces separation as the answer.

its own rejecting it. A man, like a nation, can exist 'half-slave, half-free' for only so long. Criticism of the Muslims as racists is valid, but preoccupation with criticism of the plant all too often prevents examination of the soil from which it sprang.

It is not in numbers that the Black Muslims have their greatest significance. In a nation of almost 20 million Negroes, the Muslims are numerically insignificant. The significance of the Black Muslims lies in their importance as social barometers. Theirs is a specific registering of a mood that is wide-spread, and in some ways even pervasive, in the Negro community in America—a certain anger, frustration and impatience with the Negro's situation and the rate at which it is being changed. In the nation's black ghettos there are millions who, if they cannot accept all of the Muslims' views, can sympathise with some of them and with the militancy with which they are expressed. And probably at least something of the Muslim indictment of the larger white society for its crimes against the black man hits a responsive note in the heart of every Negro—wherever he might be. The Muslims represent a particular institutionalised version of the more general mood and serve as a vehicle to communicate this mood to the larger society which all too often knows little of the hidden hurt and hidden hate of the black man.

On close examination of both the rhetoric and the teachings of the Black Muslims it becomes evident that what they are really expressing is a fundamental and deeply-felt disillusionment with the fulfilment of the American promise, and at the same time a great desire for the values that have been denied them. It is what they see as white deceit regarding matters of equality, and not a compulsive racism, that has called the Black Muslims into existence and caused them to flourish.

CONCLUSION

SEVERAL years ago the National Association for the Advancement of Colored People adopted 'Free in '63' as its motto and national objective. Now the goal seems a bit more distant. However, the day has long passed when the white American could expect the Negro to wait for his rights. Any timetable for granting Negroes' rights that does not take into account the dynamic new forces of Negro protest and the breadth of black discontent in the United States is unrealistic and doomed to failure.

To a great extent, the current restiveness in the Negro population can be attributed to the lag between the advances made in the intangible realms of law and attitude, and the lack of tangible manifestations of this progress in the average Negro's material and social position. The average Negro family income is still only 56 per cent that of the average white family. Nine years after the Supreme Court's public school desegregation decision, over 2 million Negro children still attend segregated schools. The tension which is set up between an increasingly 'liberal' social milieu and the still static economic and social position of most of the nation's Negroes causes individuals and groups to attempt to arc the gap and make the intangible more real in terms of everyday life. It is a situation such as this that calls forth a Rosa Parks or a Montgomery Improvement Association.

The lag between changes in laws and attitudes and the improvement of the individual's personal situation has also elicited another type of response. There are those for whom the increased white liberal affirmations appear as mere sham in the face of continued deprivation. For these Negroes the gap between abstract right and actual freedom is simply evidence of white America's lack of desire for an honest democracy. Promises of the coming of a 'new day' ring hollow in their ears; for them, the 'new day' that has been coming for more than 200 years is too far overdue. They will wait no longer. Unable to rationalise their position or to continue to hope for fulfilment of the American promise, they find another solution in the black nationalism of the Nation of Islam.

Both these responses display not only an unwillingness to *wait* for change, but a faith in the effectiveness of personal action as an instrument of change. The sit-in leader and the Black Muslim are both tired of waiting for their rights; it is in their solutions that they differ. The college student, with his middle-class background and American education, strives for acceptance and challenges the nation with its own Jeffersonian creed. The poorer and less educated Muslim often has little in his ghetto experience that will bolster his faith in the good intentions of the white man.

The recent surge of protest can claim a number of successes. Two hundred Southern and border cities have integrated their lunch counters. Economic boycotts have proved remarkably effective in gaining a variety of social and political demands. The power and prestige of the Federal Executive and judiciary have been swung more firmly into line as agents of equality.

In general, both as a response to protest and on its own initiative the current Administration has taken a more vigorous role in the civil rights struggle than the Federal Government has done in the past. The power of the Executive Office and the persuasion of Executive prestige have been invoked repeatedly in the cause of equality of treatment—Meredith in Mississippi being but the most obvious example. Integrationists all over the U.S.A. were greatly encouraged in November 1962 when President Kennedy signed his long-promised Executive Order prohibiting racial discrimination in federally-assisted housing. This is a highly important measure since so much of the private building in America depends on some kind of federal assistance. A significant breakthrough in the problem of racial discrimination in housing would be considered a major victory, since it is restrictive housing policies that do so much to create the ghetto and its attendant problems of overcrowded slums, social disorganisation, deterioration of educational standards and facilities, and diminution of employment opportunity. Some see a breakthrough in housing as a way out of the 'vicious circle' of discrimination.

In addition to these relatively tangible achievements in the integration of public facilities and the greater activation of the Federal Government, the protest movements have been of great educational value. They have awakened many a white to what it must mean to be a Negro in America. The Negro's self-assertion in the non-violent direct-action movement is forcing an end to the old trad-itional paternalistic relationship.

The Muslims too have met with success. The fraction of the Negro population whom they have converted has been separated from its old life into a new world structured around the temple and the Nation of Islam. Many 'marginal', deviant and criminal types of the ghetto have been rehabilitated as a result.

And what of the Negro man in the street? What does he think of all this tumult of protest? For the most part he is a member of neither the N.A.A.C.P., CORE nor the Nation of Islam. He is simply looking for something that works. He is tired of living in a 'free' land, unfree. He is probably little excited by the separationist dreams of the Muslims, but he is willing at least to consider any solution that will help him obtain the freedom that is rightfully his.

And what of the future? A. Philip Randolph, Negro President of the Pullman Car Employees of America, has observed that 'whitism breeds blackism'. The extent to which this rule will govern the future depends largely upon how fast the whole country is willing to move to eradicate its social evils. It cannot move fast enough to stem the adverse effects of discrimination; the question is, how soon before how much? Discrimination takes its toll daily in warped minds, stifled ambitions and wasted genius. Prolonged extreme oppression can only call forth extreme solutions. The direct-action phase of American Negro protest has been born and is now well established. The forms which such direct action will take in the future are not easily predictable. Undoubtedly, the Black Muslims and similar groups will continue to grow until there is little left for them to feed on. It would seem that unless America is prepared to meet the challenge of those who fight for integration today, tomorrow she will have to contend with a generation of disillusioned and discontented citizens. In the meantime, the gap between hope and reality still exists—as it has always existed for the Negro in America. However, it is evident that the voices of Negro protest will not let Americans forget that gap, or fail to remind them of the responsibility they all have in helping to close it.

SELECT BIBLIOGRAPHY

Herbert Aptheker, *American Negro Slave Revolts*, New York, Columbia University Press, 1943.

James Baldwin, *The Fire Next Time*, London, Michael Joseph, 1963.

Richard Bardolph, *The Negro Vanguard*, New York, Rinehart, 1959.

Howard Bell, 'Expressions of Negro Militancy in the North, 1840–1860', *The Journal of Negro History*, XLV, January 1960, pp. 11–20.

E. D. Beynon, ' The Voodoo Cult Among Negro Migrants in Detroit ', *The American Journal of Sociology*, XLIII, July 1937, pp. 896–911.

Francis L. Broderick, *W. E. B. DuBois: Negro Leader in a Time of Crisis*, Stanford, Stanford University Press, 1959.

Thomas Clark, *The Emerging South*, New York, Oxford University Press, 1961.

Edmund Cronon, *Black Moses: The Story of Marcus Garvey and the Universal Negro Improvement Association*, Madison, University of Wisconsin Press, 1955.

Frederick Douglass, *Narrative of the Life of Frederick Douglass An American Slave*, ed. Benjamin Quarles, Cambridge (Mass.), Harvard University Press, 1960.

W. E. B. Du Bois, *The Souls of Black Folk*, Greenwich, Premier Americana, Fawcett Publications, 1961.

Stanley M. Elkins, *Slavery: A Problem in American Institutional and Intellectual Life*, Chicago, Chicago University Press, 1959.

E. U. Essien-Udom, *Black Nationalism*, London, Oxford University Press, 1962.

John Hope Franklin, *From Slavery to Freedom*, New York, Knopf, 1956.

Thomas Gaither, 'Jailed-In', Congress of Racial Equality, New York, 1961.

'Have Organisations Helped?', New York, N.A.A.C.P., reprinted from *The Catholic Digest*, August 1957.

Nat Hentoff, 'Elijah in the Wilderness', *The Reporter*, 4 August 1960, pp. 37–40.

'How Two Negroes Campaign for Congress in Mississippi', *Jet*, 25 January 1962, pp. 18–21.

Langston Hughes, *Fight for Freedom: The Story of the N.A.A.C.P.*, New York, Norton, 1962.

'In Your Midst—Mr. Elijah Muhammad', Black Muslim publication.

Robert Jack, *The History of the N.A.A.C.P.*, Boston, Meador Publishing Co., 1943.

Martin Luther King, Jr., *Stride Toward Freedom*, New York, Harper, 1958.

James H. Laue, *Race Relations Revolution: The Sit-In Movement*, Unpublished thesis, Harvard University, 1961.

C. Eric Lincoln, *The Black Muslims in America*, Boston, Beacon Press, 1961.

—— 'Strategy of a Sit-In', *The Reporter*, 5 January 1961, pp. 20–3.

Louis E. Lomax, *The Negro Revolt*, London, Hamish Hamilton, 1963.

Benjamin Mintz, with Richard Spenser and Joseph B. Robison, *Assault Upon Freedom of Association*, New York, American Jewish Congress, 1957.

Gunnar Myrdal, *An American Dilemma*, New York, Harper, 1944.

N.A.A.C.P.—An American Organisation, New York, N.A.A.C.P., 1960.

Mary White Ovington, *The Walls Came Tumbling Down*, New York, Harcourt, Brace, 1947.

Barbara Ann Posey, *Why I Sit In*, New York, N.A.A.C.P., Reprinted from *Datebook Magazine*, 1960.

S.C.L.C., *Southern Christian Leadership Conference*, Atlanta, 1960.

Southern Regional Council, *The Student Protest Movement, Winter, 1960*, Special Report SRC-13, 1 April 1960 (Revised).

—— *The Freedom Ride*, Special Report SRC-20, 30 May 1961.

Samuel R. Spencer, *Booker T. Washington and the Negro's Place in American Life*, Boston, Little, Brown, 1955.

Warren D. St. James, *The National Association for the Advancement of Colored People: A Case Study in Pressure Groups*, New York, The Exposition Press, 1958.

United States Civil Rights Commission, *Freedom to the Free: 1863–1963 Century of Emancipation*, Washington, 1963.

Daniel Walder, 'The Contemporary Opposition to the Political and Educational Ideals of Booker T. Washington', *The Journal of Negro History*, XLV, April 1960, pp. 103–115.

Booker T. Washington, *Up From Slavery*, New York, Doubleday, Page, 1900.

Clark Woodroe, 'S.N.C.C. and the New South', *The Harvard Crimson Review*, 16 February 1962, pp. 11–12.

C. Vann Woodward, *Origins of the New South*, Baton Rouge, University of Louisiana Press, 1951.

— *The Strange Career of Jim Crow*, New York, Oxford University Press, 1955, revised edition 1957.

William Worthy, 'The Angriest Negroes', *Esquire*, February 1961, pp. 101–105.